National Curriculum
English
Practice Book for

Year 5

◨ SCHOLASTIC

Book End, Range Road, Witney, Oxfordshire, OX29 0YD
www.scholastic.co.uk

© 2014, Scholastic Ltd

5 6 7 8 9   8 9 0 1 2 3

British Library Cataloguing-in-Publication Data
A catalogue record for this book is available from the British Library.

ISBN 978-1407-12898-6
Printed by Malaysia

Editorial
Rachel Morgan, Melissa Somers, Sarah Sodhi and Catherine Baker

Design
Scholastic Design Team: Neil Salt, Nicolle Thomas
and Oxford Designers & Illustrators Ltd

Cover Design
Neil Salt

Illustration
Thomas Giovanis

Acknowledgements
The publishers gratefully acknowledge permission to reproduce the following
copyright material: **Kevin Crossley-Holland** for the use of an extract from
"Room for one more" by Kevin Crossley-Holland © 1998, Kevin Crossley-
Holland (1998, Oxford University Press). **Brian Moses** for the use of 'The
Lost Angels' by Brian Moses from "Behind the Staffroom Door: The Very
Best of Brian Moses" by Brian Moses © 1998, Brian Moses (2007, Macmillan
Children's Books). **Kit Wright** for the use of 'My dad, your dad' by Kit Wright
from "Rabbiting On" by Kit Wright © 1978, Kit Wright (1978, Collins). **Her
Majesty's Stationery Office** for the use of an extract from "What you
need to know about driving licences" (D100) produced by the DVLA © 2005,
Crown copyright and 'What is a visa?' from the Foreign and Commonwealth
Office website http://www.ukvisas.gov.uk/ © 2005, Crown copyright. Crown
copyright material is reproduced with the permission of the Controller of
HMSO and the Queen's Printer for Scotland. **The Society of Authors** for the
use of 'Hints on Pronunciation for Foreigners' by George Bernard Shaw. Poem
© 1965, George Bernard Shaw (1965, Sunday Times Letters). Every effort has
been made to trace copyright holders for the works reproduced in this book,
and the publishers apologise for any inadvertent omissions.

Contents

Why buy this book?

The *100 Practice Activities* series has been designed to support the National Curriculum in schools in England. The curriculum is challenging in English and includes the requirement for children's understanding to be secure before moving on. These practice books will help your child practise all of the skills they will learn at school, including some topics they might not have encountered previously.

How to use this book

- The content is divided into National Curriculum topics (for example, Spelling, Grammar, Comprehension and so on). Find out what your child is doing in school and dip into the relative practice activities as required.

- Let your child know you are sharing the activities and support if necessary using the helpful quick tips at the top of most pages.

- Keep the working time short and come back to an activity if your child finds it too difficult. Ask your child to note any areas of difficulty. Don't worry if your child does not 'get' a concept first time, as children learn at different rates and content is likely to be covered throughout the school year.

- Check your child's answers using the answers section on www.scholastic.co.uk/100practice/englishy5

- You will also find additional interactive activities for your child to play on the website.

- Give lots of encouragement and tick off the progress chart as your child completes each chapter.

How to use the book

This is the title of the activity.

This tells you which topic you're working on.

Letters in slashes (like this) tell you it's the sound and not the spelling.

These boxes will help you with the activity.
(If there's not one on your page, go back and find the last one.)

This is the instruction text. It tells you what to do.

Follow the instruction to complete the activity.

You might have to write on lines, in boxes, draw or circle things.

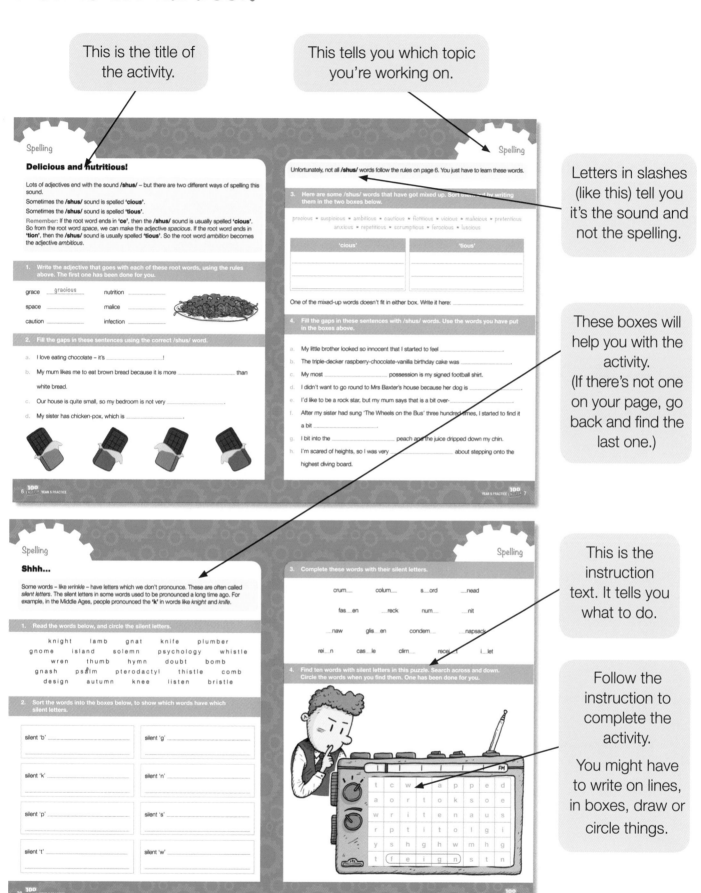

If you need help, ask an adult!

Delicious and nutritious!

Lots of adjectives end with the sound **/shus/** – but there are two different ways of spelling this sound.

Sometimes the **/shus/** sound is spelled **'cious'**.

Sometimes the **/shus/** sound is spelled **'tious'**.

Remember: If the root word ends in **'ce'**, then the **/shus/** sound is usually spelled **'cious'**. So from the root word *space*, we can make the adjective *spacious*. If the root word ends in **'tion'**, then the **/shus/** sound is usually spelled **'tious'**. So the root word *ambition* becomes the adjective *ambitious*.

1. **Write the adjective that goes with each of these root words, using the rules above. The first one has been done for you.**

grace _____gracious_____   nutrition _____

space _____   malice _____

caution _____   infection _____

2. **Fill the gaps in these sentences using the correct /shus/ word.**

a.   I love eating chocolate – it's _____!

b.   My mum likes me to eat brown bread because it is more _____ than

white bread.

c.   Our house is quite small, so my bedroom is not very _____.

d.   My sister has chicken-pox, which is _____.

Unfortunately, not all **/shus/** words follow the rules on page 6. You just have to learn these words.

3. Here are some /shus/ words that have got mixed up. Sort them out by writing them in the two boxes below.

precious * suspicious * ambitious * cautious * fictitious * vicious * malicious * pretentious
anxious * repetitious * scrumptious * ferocious * luscious

'cious'	'tious'
_____	_____
_____	_____
_____	_____

One of the mixed-up words doesn't fit in either box. Write it here: _____

4. Fill the gaps in these sentences with /shus/ words. Use the words you have put in the boxes above.

a. My little brother looked so innocent that I started to feel _____.

b. The triple-decker raspberry-chocolate-vanilla birthday cake was _____.

c. My most _____ possession is my signed football shirt.

d. I didn't want to go round to Mrs Baxter's house because her dog is _____.

e. I'd like to be a rock star, but my mum says that is a bit over-_____.

f. After my sister had sung 'The Wheels on the Bus' three hundred times, I started to find it

a bit _____.

g. I bit into the _____ peach and the juice dripped down my chin.

h. I'm scared of heights, so I was very _____ about stepping onto the

highest diving board.

Spelling

Special and essential

The words *special* and *essential* both end with the same **/shul/** sound – but they are not spelled in quite the same way. Some **/shul/** words end with **'cial'**, like *special* – and others end with **'tial'**, like *essential*.

Remember: When the letter before the **/shul/** ending is a vowel, we usually use **'cial'**. For example: sp**e**cial, off**i**cial.

When the letter before the **/shul/** ending is a consonant, we usually use 'tial'. For example: esse**n**tial, confide**n**tial.

1. **Have a go! Add the right /shul/ ending to each of these words, using the rules above. The first one has been done for you.**

a.   spec ial_____

b.   par _____

c.   essen _____

d.   offi _____

e.   poten _____

f.   impar _____

g.   so _____

h.   benefi _____

2. **Fill the gaps in these sentences using some of the 'shul' words you have written above. Look the words up in a dictionary if you are not sure of the meanings.**

a.   Max is brilliant at football – our coach says he has a lot of _____!

b.   Mum had to fill in an _____ form when she wanted to get a new passport.

c.   The dentist says it is _____ that I brush my teeth every

night and morning without fail.

d.   My two friends asked me to sort out an argument for them, but I couldn't take sides –

I had to stay _____

e.   I hate long walks, but my dad says they are _____ for my health.

There are some **/shul/** words which don't follow the rules on page 8. You just have to learn how to spell these words.

3. Here are some 'shul' words that don't follow the spelling rules. Sort them out by writing them in the two boxes below.

palatial * financial * provincial * initial * spatial * commercial

'cial'	'tial'
_____ _____	_____ _____
_____	_____

4. Use the words in the boxes to fill the gaps in these sentences. Look the words up in a dictionary if you are not sure of the meanings.

a. The headteacher's house was enormous – it was really _____!

b. My dad keeps bumping into things. Mum says he has poor _____ awareness.

c. Elliot's middle _____ is X. He says it stands for Xavier.

d. English cities other than London are sometimes called _____ cities.

e. I have spent all my pocket money for the next six weeks, so now I have a bit of a _____ problem.

f. Sometimes the _____s are better than the programmes on TV.

5. Pick a 'tial' word and a 'cial' word from the list below. Write a sentence using the words.

special * palatial * essential * initial * official * financial

_____

_____

Ant machine

Look at this word: *important.* Can you spot the **'ant'** at the end?
The machine below turns root words into new words, ending with **'ant'**, **'ance'**, **'ancy'** or **'ation'**. Some root words will make new words with most or all of these endings.

Remember: Not all root words will give you a real word in each box of the ant machine. Use a dictionary to check your words if you're not sure whether they are real.

1. Have a go! Try putting the root words below into the 'ant' machine. Write the root words in, and see how many new real words you can make. The first one has been done for you.

~~import~~ ✳ observ ✳ hesit ✳ expect ✳ toler ✳ relev ✳ ten ✳ assist

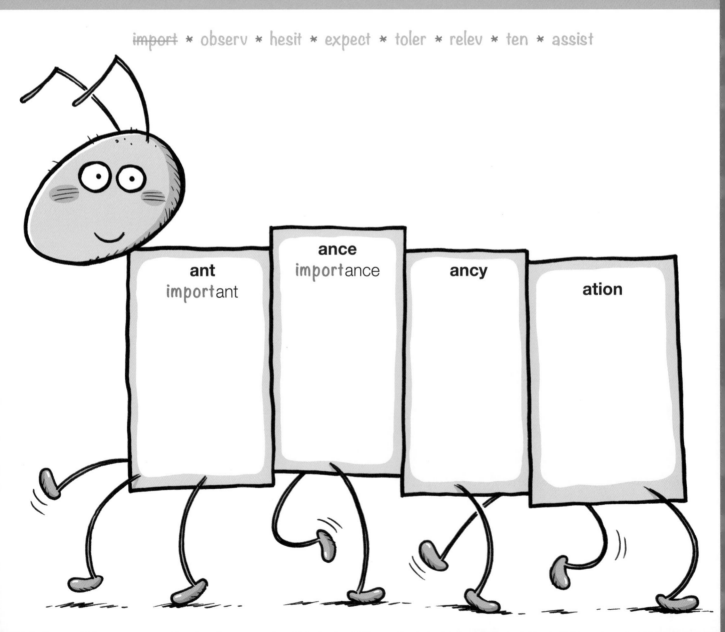

ant
important

ance
importance

ancy

ation

2. Read the sentences below, and draw a ring round the right 'ant', 'ance', 'ancy' or 'ation' word to complete each sentence. Watch out: some of the options are not real words. You need to check that the sentence makes sense, so use your dictionary if you are not sure.

a. Tom always kept his eyes open for clues – he was a very **observant** / **observance** / **observancy** / **observation** boy.

b. There was a long **hesitant** / **hesitance** / **hesitancy** / **hesitation** before Joel answered the difficult maths question.

c. I discovered a strange, sticky **substant** / **substance** / **substancy** / **substation** in the bottom of my pocket.

d. I tried to get into the changing cubicle but there was already an **occupant** / **occupance** / **occupancy** / **occupation** inside it.

e. My bedroom is always very untidy, so it's lucky my mum is quite **tolerant** / **tolerance** / **tolerancy** / **toleration**.

f. Janna had a strong **expectant** / **expectance** / **expectancy** / **expectation** that she would get a new bike for her birthday.

Here is a word cluster for the root 'occup', with the endings 'ant', 'ancy' and 'ation'. (There is no 'ance' this time because *occupance* is not a real word.)

3. Write the word clusters for the roots 'observ', 'expect' and 'assist', using the endings 'ant', 'ance', 'ancy' and 'ation'. Remember: You won't need all of the endings for each root.

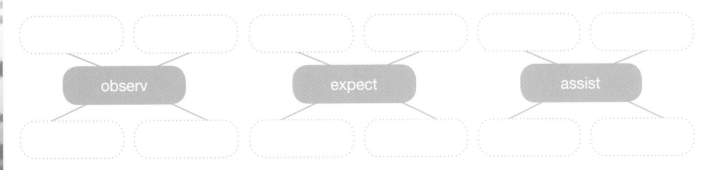

Ent machine

Look at this word: *frequent*. Can you spot the **'ent'** at the end?

The machine below turns root words into new words, ending with **'ent'**, **'ence'**, **'ency'**.

Some root words will make new words with most or all of these endings. Others will only make words with one or two of the endings.

If you put the root word 'frequ' into the 'ent' machine, it makes two new words – *frequent* and *frequency*.

---

1. **Try putting the root words below into the 'ent' machine. Write the root words in, and see how many new real words you can make.**

innoc * dec * confid * obedi * independ * evid * differ

ent

ence

ency

2. Read the sentences below, and draw a ring round the right 'ent', 'ence', 'ency' word to complete each sentence. Watch out: some of the options are not real words. You need to check that the sentence makes sense, so use your dictionary if you are not sure.

a. As I entered the darkened room, I was aware of a strange **present** / **presence** / **presency**.

b. Anna loves singing and acting, and she is very **confident** / **confidence** / **confidency** on stage.

c. Mr Moore put up his hand and called for **silent** / **silence** / **silency**.

d. My dog, Rocket, always goes and gets his lead when it is time for a walk, which shows he is quite **intelligent** / **intelligence** / **intelligency**.

e. Ellie always tries to stop fights in the playground, because she doesn't believe in **violent** / **violence** / **violency**.

f. The baker had to knead the dough for a long time to get it to the right **consistent** / **consistence** / **consistency**.

Here is a word cluster for the root 'ag', with the endings 'ent' and 'ency'. (There is no 'ence' this time because *agence* is not a real word.)

3. Write the word clusters for the roots 'compet', 'resid' and 'dec', using the endings 'ent', 'ence' and 'ency'. Remember: You won't need all of the endings for each root:

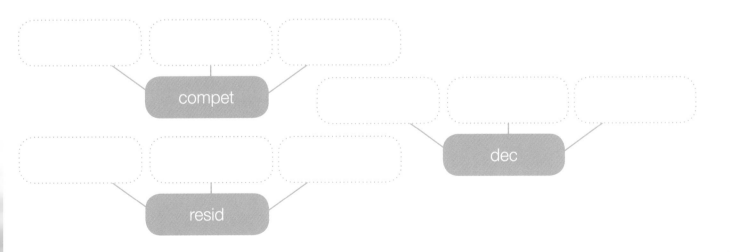

Are you able?

Lots of words end in **'able'** or **'ably'**. Look at these examples:

- *considerable – considerably*
- *adorable – adorably*
- *applicable – applicably*

Some words have endings that sound like these, but are spelled **'ible'** or **'ibly'**. For example

- *possible – possibly*
- *visible – visibly*

So how do you decide whether a word ends in **'able'**/**'ably'** or **'ible'**/**'ibly'**? Luckily, there is a rule that helps. If there is a word with the same root, ending in **'ation'**, then we normally use the **'able'**/**'ably'** spelling.

That means that if you are wondering how to spell *considerable*, you can think of the word *consideration* – and that tells you that it must end in **'able'**, not in **'ible'**.

---

1. **Use the 'ation' rule above to help you fill in this chart.**

Which spelling is right?	Is there an 'ation' word?	So is it 'able' or 'ible'?	So is it 'ably' or 'ibly'?
sensable or *sensible*	No – sensiblation is not a real word	sensible	sensibly
adorable or *adorible*	Yes – adoration	adorable	adorably
possable or *possible*			
applicable or *applicible*			
incredable or *incredible*			
terrable or *terrible*			
visable or *visible*			

The **'ation'** rule mentioned on page 14 doesn't always help if you want to work out whether a word is spelled **'able'** or **'ible'**. There are lots of **'able'** words that don't have a linked **'ation'** word using the same root. For example, we say:

- *comfortable* but not *comfortation*
- *reasonable* but not *reasonation*
- *enjoyable* but not *enjoyation.*

The rule for these words is: Can you hear a whole root word before the **'able'** ending? If so, then use **'able'**, not **'ible'**.

Say the word *comfortable* out loud. You can hear the word *comfort* before the **'able'** ending – so you know that the ending is spelled **'able'**, not **'ible'**.

2. Use the *say it out loud* rule above to help you fill in this chart.

Which spelling is right?	Can you hear a whole root word before the 'able'/'ible' ending?	So is it 'able' or 'ible'?	So is it 'ably' or 'ibly'?
reliable or *reliible*	Yes – you can hear the word 'rely', although the 'y' changes to 'i'	reliable	reliably
horrable or *horrible*	No – 'horr' is not a whole root word	horrible	horribly
reasonable or *reasonible*			
intelligable or *intelligible*			
legable or *legible*			
dependable or *dependible*			
terrable or *terrible*			
visable or *visible*			

Spelling

Fillable gaps

Choose the correct word endings to fill the gaps in the sentences below. You can choose from **'ible'**, **'able'**, **'ibly'** or **'ably'**. Look back at the rules on pages 14 and 15 if you need a clue about which to use.

1. Write the correct word endings to finish these sentences.

a.   When I went to Nan's house, I found her dozing in a comfort_____ chair.

b.   Nina thought her pet alligator, Binky, was ador_____.

c.   "Enjoy your spelling homework!" said Miss Batey. "Huh!" I thought. "That's imposs_____."

d.   Dan got to the top of the mountain consider_____ faster than the others.

e.   It was terr_____ cold in the classroom.

f.   I've got the most incred_____ bruise on my knee – it's purple, orange and yellow.

g.   "Could you poss_____ pass me the tomato ketchup?" asked Gavin politely.

h.   Jamie loved his pet dog, Jasper, because he was so depend_____.

i.   Hitesh came into school with bright pink hair yesterday. It was a shock, because he's

usually so sens_____.

j.   I loved the chocolate cake we had for tea, but the cabbage soup was horr_____.

k.   Our car keeps breaking down – Dad says it's not very reli_____.

l.   Although I wasn't looking forward to doing my homework, I actually found it

reason_____ enjoy_____.

m.   I asked for a big slice of cake, but the one I got was so small it was almost invis_____.

2. Read the sentences below. Write the correct word from the list to fill each gap.

enjoyable * enjoyably * possibly * possible * sensibly * sensible
considerably * considerable

a. My big sister is usually quite _____, but for some reason today she is

standing on her head, waggling her legs in the air and singing at the top of her voice.

b. Mum gave me a big bowl of chocolate mousse, which was _____

sweet and sticky.

c. This may _____ be the best day of my life.

d. I am _____ taller than Matthew, even though he is a year older than me.

e. Mum thought I was going to lose my mobile, but I _____ put it in my bag.

f. We went to the seaside for the day, but it was not very _____ because it

was too cold and rainy to go on the beach.

g. It took Aidan a _____ amount of time to finish the last level of the game.

h. It's _____ that my friend Josh might come round this afternoon.

3. Sort the root words into the correct box, depending on whether they end in 'able'/'ably' or 'ible'/'ibly'. Two have been done for you.

depend * incred * ador * poss * applic * consider * enjoy
reli * understand * reason * terr * comfort

'able'/'ably'	'ible'/'ibly'
dependable, dependably	incredible, incredibly
_____	_____
_____	_____
_____	_____
_____	_____
_____	_____
_____	_____

No stress!

When you add a suffix to a root word that ends with **'fer'**, sometimes you have to double the final **'r'**, like this: *refer – referring – referred.*

But sometimes, you don't have to double the **'r'** when you add a suffix to this kind of word. For example: *refer – reference – referee.*

How can you work out whether the **'r'** needs to be doubled or not? Luckily, there is a simple rule. If the **'fer'** syllable is stressed after you add the suffix, then you double the **'r'**. If the **'fer'** syllable *isn't* stressed, then you don't double the **'r'**. (If you say *referring* out loud, you will hear that the **'fer'** syllable is stressed, or said with extra emphasis. If you say *referee* out loud, you will hear that the extra emphasis is on the **'ee'** syllable, not on the **'fer'** syllable.)

1.   Complete the table, making sure you follow the rule.

Root	Suffix	New word
prefer	ing	
prefer	ed	
prefer	ence	
transfer	ing	
transfer	ed	
transfer	ence	
defer	ing	
defer	ed	
defer	ence	
infer	ing	
infer	ed	
infer	ence	

In some words ending with **'fer'**, the **'fer'** syllable is never stressed.
For example, we don't stress **'fer'** in any of these words: *offer – offered – offering*.

So in words like this, we don't double the **'r'** when we add a suffix.

2. Fill in the New word column, making sure you follow the rules. Watch out: sometimes the 'r' needs to be doubled, and sometimes it doesn't.

Root	Suffix	New word
differ	ence	
differ	ed	
pilfer	ing	
pilfer	ed	
transfer	ed	
transfer	ence	
suffer	ing	
suffer	ed	
defer	ing	
infer	ing	
proffer	ed	

3. What does *pilfer* mean? Look it up in a dictionary if you're not sure.

a. Write a definition of *pilfer.* _____

b. What does *proffer* mean? Look this up too, if you need to. Then write a definition.

_____

c. Choose one of these two words and use it in a sentence. You can add a suffix if you like.

_____

Prefixes with hyphens

Normally when we add a prefix to a root word, we stick the prefix on to the front of the word without a hyphen, like this: *re + position = reposition*

However, sometimes we need to put a hyphen between the prefix and the root word. Usually we do this when the prefix ends in a vowel, and the root word begins with the same vowel. For example:
re + enter = re-enter, not *reenter*
co + owner = co-owner, not *coowner*

Adding a hyphen to words like these makes them easier to pronounce and to understand.

Normally, if the prefix ends with a vowel and the root word starts with a different vowel, you don't need to add a hyphen. For example:
pro + active = proactive, not *pro-active*

But some prefixes always have a hyphen after them, whatever the root word is like. For example, you always need a hyphen with these prefixes:
'ex' – *ex-soldier*
'self' – *self-portrait*
'all' – *all-encompassing*

1. Use the rules above to help you fill in this chart.

Prefix	Root word	New word
re	active	reactive
ex	husband	
co	habit	
re	enact	
co	operate	
all	inclusive	
self	respect	
pre	enrolment	
pre	date	

2. Using the rules on page 20, see how many new words you can make out of the prefixes and root words in the boxes below. They don't have to be real words – but they must follow the rules about using hyphens.

Prefixes
ex * all * co * semi * pre self * dis * un * re

Root words
husband * friend * enveloping * able appointment * industrial * enactment ordinated * invalid * eminent expected * obsessed

Write your new words here.

_____

_____

_____

_____

3. Choose three of the real words that you made. (If you didn't make any real words, have another look at the prefixes and root words and see if you can find three real ones.) Write a sentence using each of these three real words.

_____

_____

_____

_____

_____

_____

Spelling

Except after 'c'

Write **'ie'** when it is a long **/ee/** sound, except after **'c'** when you should write **'ei'**.
Examples: *chief, field, shield, ceiling, deceive, receive.*
Exceptions: *either, height, leisure, neither, seize, their, weird.*

Write **'ei'** when the sound is not a long **/ee/** sound, especially when the sound is long **'a'** (**/ay/**).
Examples: *eight, freight, height, neighbour, reign, weigh.*
Exceptions: *friend, mischief.*

1.   Add 'ie' or 'ei' in the gaps below.

ach____ve	bes____ge	th____r
p____rce	rel____f	h____ght
gr____f	rec____ve	f____rce
c____ling	w____gh	s____ze
____ght	f____ld	____ther

2. Use some of the words you made on page 22 to fill the gaps in these sentences.

a. I don't like _____ cabbage

or broccoli.

b. Fifty feathers _____ less

than ten pennies.

c. Mum gave me a lot of _____

because I lost my PE kit.

d. I hope one day I will _____

my ambition to travel to Mars.

e. Our cat, Tiddles, looks gentle – but really she is very _____.

f. Jamie looked up at the _____ in terror: there was a giant spider

dangling right above him!

g. What a _____! I managed to get home before the bullies caught up with me.

h. Jamal hopes to _____ a new video game for his birthday.

i. Opposite our holiday cottage was a _____ with a herd of cows in it.

j. Dad measured my _____ yesterday and I found out I had grown

five centimetres!

3. Write sentences using each of these 'ei' words. Look them up in the dictionary first, if you're not sure what they mean.

deceive * perceive * conceited * receipt

_____

_____

_____

_____

_____

Pronunciation variations

English spelling is only partly phonetic. Many spellings are based on meaning – for example, *electricity* is spelled to show its relationship with *electric*. Many spellings have changed over time – for example, in the Middle Ages, every letter of *knight* was pronounced. As a result, English is not the easiest language to learn!

1. **Read and enjoy the poem.**

2. **Highlight or underline all the difficult spellings.**

I take it you already know
Of tough and bough and cough and dough?
Others may stumble but not you
On hiccough, thorough, lough and through.
Well done! And now you wish perhaps
To learn the less familiar traps.

Beware of heard, a dreadful word,
That looks like beard and sounds like bird;
And dead, it's said like bed not bead –
For goodness' sake don't call it deed!
Watch out for meat and great and threat
(They rhyme with suite and straight and debt).

A moth is not a moth in mother,
Nor both in bother, broth in brother;
And here is not a match for there,
Nor dear and fear for bear and pear,
And then there's dose and rose and lose –
Just look at them – and goose and choose;

And cork and work and card and ward,
And font and front, and word and sword,
And do and go, then thwart and cart.
Come, come I've hardly made a start.
A dreadful language? Man alive,
I'd mastered it when I was five.

George Bernard Shaw

The English language is full of unusual spellings and pronunciations, but the letter string **'ough'** is particularly tricky. It can be pronounced in lots of different ways.

3. Look back at the first verse of the poem on page 24. Write all the 'ough' words in the chart below. Then think of a word that rhymes with each of these words. Your rhyming words probably won't have the letter string 'ough'.

Clue: *hiccough* is an old-fashioned spelling of *hiccup*.

lough is an old-fashioned spelling of *loch*.

'ough' word from the poem	Rhyming word

4. Use the 'ough' words from the chart to fill the gaps in the sentences below.

a. The branch of a tree is sometimes called a _____.

b. I started to _____ loudly, but when I held my breath, it stopped.

c. Jason's route home took him _____ the local park.

d. When you are brushing your teeth, you have to be _____.

e. Amelie isn't at school today, because she has a nasty _____.

f. Dobbo thinks he's _____, but really he's just a pathetic bully.

g. Bread and buns are made from _____.

It's tough!

Some **'ough'** words are pronounced in the same way as each other.

1. **Look at the 'ough' words below, and write them in the correct boxes to show how they are pronounced.**

plough * though * thought * brought * rough * enough * nought
Slough * although * cough * ought * trough * tough * thorough
dough * borough * bought * fought * through

'ough' sounds like 'or' as in *fort*

_____

_____

'ough' sounds like 'oo' as in *moon*

_____

'ough' sounds like 'er' as in *manner*

_____

'ough' sounds like 'uff' as in *cuff*

_____

'ough' sounds like 'ow' as in *now*

_____

'ough' sounds like 'off' as in *toffee*

_____

'ough' sounds like 'ow' as in *snow*

_____

2. **Pick three 'ough' words with different pronunciations, and write a sentence using each word.**

_____

_____

_____

3. **Written below are some extracts from WPC Clough's diary, after she was called to the scene of an accident. Supply the vital missing words. (Clue: they all contain the letter pattern 'ough'.) Think of all the words you can with 'ough' in them first to help you.**

Question 1   Have you always lived in _____, madam?

Question 2   Which _____ was it exactly that the cradle fell from?

Question 3   Was there not a _____ branch to put the cradle on?

Question 4   The neighbours tell me they heard the baby _____ and

spluttering just before the incident. Is that so?

Question 5   Do you now believe you _____ to have stayed outside near

the baby?

Question 6   Had the field been _____ recently? Yes? What a good job

or the baby would have had a very _____ landing.

Well, that's _____ for now, thank you, madam. Make sure

you take more care in future.

Have you guessed which nursery rhyme this was based on? Write it below.

_____

Spelling

Shhh...

Some words – like *wrinkle* – have letters which we don't pronounce. These are often called *silent letters*. The silent letters in some words used to be pronounced a long time ago. For example, in the Middle Ages, people pronounced the **'k'** in words like *knight* and *knife*.

1. Read the words below, and circle the silent letters.

knight   lamb   gnat   knife   plumber

gnome   island   solemn   psychology   whistle

wren   thumb   hymn   doubt   bomb

gnash   psalm   pterodactyl   thistle   comb

design   autumn   knee   listen   bristle

2. Sort the words into the boxes below, to show which words have which silent letters.

silent 'b' _____

silent 'g' _____

silent 'k' _____

silent 'n' _____

silent 'p' _____

silent 's' _____

silent 't' _____

silent 'w' _____

3. Complete these words with their silent letters.

crum___   colum___   s___ord   ___nead

fas___en   ___reck   num___   ___nit

___naw   glis___en   condem___   ___napsack

rei___n   cas___le   clim___   recei___t   i___let

4. Find ten words with silent letters in this puzzle. Search across and down. Circle the words when you find them. One has been done for you.

t	c	w	r	a	p	p	e	d
a	o	r	t	o	k	s	o	e
w	r	i	t	e	n	a	u	s
r	p	t	i	t	o	l	g	i
y	s	h	g	h	w	m	h	g
t	f	e	i	g	n	s	t	n

Good advice

The pair of words below sound alike, but they are spelled slightly differently.

- *advice* is a noun: *Let me give you some good advice.*
- *advise* is a verb: *I advise you to avoid the snail and avocado stew.*

With this pair of words, it's quite easy to remember which spelling is which, because the verb *advise* ends with a sound like **'z'**. It can't be spelled with a **'c'**, so we know this word must use **'s'**.

Here's another pair of words like this:

- *device* is a noun: *Dad invented a strange robotic device to wash the car for him.*
- *devise* is a verb: *Sadly it didn't work, so Dad had to devise another way of washing the car.*

There are other pairs of words that also work like this – where the noun has a **'c'** and the verb has an **'s'**. Pronunciation isn't much help with these words, though, because they sound the same.

- *practice* is a noun: *I want to be a rapper, so I have to do a lot of practice.*
- *practise* is a verb: *Mum has asked me not to practise my rapping when Gran's here.*
- *licence* is a noun: *If you want to go fishing for salmon, you need a rod licence.*
- *license* is a verb: *Luckily I am licensed for fishing already.*

---

1.   Read these sentences and add the missing letters. Remember: 'c' for a noun, 's' for a verb.

a.   Jamal's not back yet because he has football practi__e on Wednesdays.

b.   Are you licen__ed to do that?

c.   A mobile phone is a very useful devi__e.

d.   Mrs Cooper advi__ed me to put my gloves on before going out in the snow.

e.   The children devi__ed a plan for their sports day events.

f.   You have to practi__e if you want to get better at mental maths.

g.   You don't need a licen__e to own a pet rabbit.

Here's one way to remember whether to use *practice* or *practise* in a sentence, or *licence* or *license*. Try swapping the tricky word in the sentence for *advice/advise*, and see which makes better sense. For example:

* *I wish Dad would stop his trombone practice/practise.*

Take out trombone practice/practise and fill the gap with advice/advise:

* *I wish Dad would stop his advise.*

That doesn't make sense – the sentence sounds wrong.

* *I wish Dad would stop his advice.*

That does make sense, so we know that *practice* must be spelled with a **'c'** in this sentence, like *advice*.

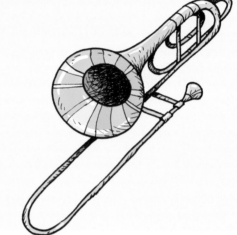

---

2. **Fill the gaps in the these sentences with the words below. You won't need to use all the words.**

practice * practise * practised * practising * advice * advise * advised * advising
licence * license * licensed * licensing * device * devise * devised * devising

a. I saw a notice _____ people not to go into the river because of

the alligators.

b. My big brother has already got his provisional driving _____. He had

to apply to the Driver and Vehicle _____ Agency before he could start

having driving lessons.

c. However hard I _____, I'll never be able to sing as well as Anna.

d. I have _____ a cunning plan to get out of tidying my bedroom.

e. I have invented a _____ that tidies up automatically.

f. Michael gave me some good _____: never eat anything that is bigger

than your head.

g. Miss Ackroyd has broken her leg, so dance _____ is cancelled.

h. Dad has been _____ the trombone for over ten years now, but sadly

he is still rubbish at it.

Spelling

There's another noun/verb pair of words that sound alike and follow the same rule: **'c'** for a noun, and **'s'** for a verb. However, this pair is a bit different:

- *prophe**c**y* is a noun: *There was an ancient **prophecy** that the world would end last Monday.*
- *prophe**s**y* is a verb: *Fortunately, although the disaster was **prophesied**, it didn't happen.*

So now you know five noun/verb pairs like this, which all use the rule of **'c'** for a noun, and **'s'** for a verb: *advice/advise, device/devise, practice/practise, licence/license, prophecy/prophesy.*

3. Circle the correct word or words in each sentence below.

a. Gran gave me a piece of **advice** / **advise** that I have never forgotten.

b. She **adviced** / **advised** me always to wear earplugs when I **practice** / **practise** playing the bagpipes.

c. She **prophecied** / **prophesied** that if I forgot to do this, terrible things might happen.

d. She even **deviced** / **devised** an ingenious **device** / **devise** to remind me to put my earplugs in.

e. Gran knew that if I kept up with the **practice** / **practise**, one day I could be a **licenced** / **licensed** bagpipe player.

f. However, one sad day, I forgot Gran's excellent **advice** / **advise**.

g. I did my bagpipe **practice** / **practise** without wearing earplugs.

h. Gran's gloomy **prophecy** / **prophesy** came true, and now I am the only deaf piper in all of London.

4. Write some sentences of your own to show that you know how to use these words correctly. You can change the endings of the verbs if you like.

advice: _____

advise: _____

practice: _____

practise: _____

How much farther, Father?

The words *farther* and *father* are *homophones*: they are spelled differently, and they have different meanings, but they sound the same. *Farther* means *further*. *Father* is another name for *dad*.
Homophones are often used in jokes like the ones you find in Christmas crackers.
Here's an example:

Q When is a bucket unwell?
A When it is a little pail.

---

1. Solve the clues below with one word, and then match the word to its homophone. The first one is done for you.

Clues	Answers	Homophones
To leave quickly	*flee*	serial
A male parent		heard
Eat a bowl of this for breakfast		guessed
A visitor		flea
A group of animals		draft
A cold current of air		farther

---

2. Use the words *father* and *farther* to fill the gaps in the sentences below.

a. Dan's _____ is a firefighter.

b. It was getting dark as we wandered _____ and _____ into the woods.

c. I asked my _____ how much _____ we had to go.

d. Did your _____ never tell you that it's rude to do that?

e. I managed to run 5km, but my _____ ran even _____.

I'll go to the isle

There are three *homophones* that sound like **/ile/**:

- *I'll* meaning *I will*
- *aisle* meaning a path or gangway between seats
- *isle* meaning a small island.

1. Choose the correct homophone to fill the gaps in the sentences below.

a. The church was empty as I walked down the _____ between the pews.

b. We sailed across the lake to the little _____ in the middle.

c. I think _____ have fish fingers for tea.

d. _____ go to the _____ of Wight for my holidays this year.

e. I tried to get to the door of the train, but a suitcase was blocking the _____.

f. _____ show you the _____ where the seals and puffins live.

2. Two of these sentences have the correct homophone. Tick the boxes to show which ones.

a. The little aisle far out to sea was shrouded in mist. ☐

b. We had been sailing for days when a tiny isle came into view. ☐

c. I'll go with you to the I'll of Skye. ☐

d. My brother barged down the aisle of the plane without looking where he was going. ☐

e. My brother had a window seat, but I had the I'll seat. ☐

f. The bride walked proudly down the isle of the church. ☐

Thinking allowed

Here is another pair of words that are easily confused:

- *aloud* means out loud.
- *allowed* means permitted.

To help you work out which spelling is which, remember that *allowed* is a verb, and it ends with **'ed'**. *Aloud* is not a verb, so it doesn't have a verb ending.

It can also be hard to know when to use the two words *affect* and *effect*.

- **a**ffect is normally a verb: *If I haven't had enough sleep, it **affects** my mood badly.*
- **e**ffect is normally a noun: *A lack of sleep has a bad **effect** on my mood.*

1. Use these four words to fill the gaps in the sentences below.

a. The snow has _____ our travel plans – we won't be able to go by car.

b. You're not _____ to come round to my house for a sleepover.

c. Don't just think about the poem – say it _____.

d. Jake's friendly smile has a big _____ on everyone he meets.

2. Solve the clues to fill in this mini-crossword.

Across

1. Our holiday plans were ____ by the train strike.
3. We were reading ____ in class.
4. Tom's angry words had no ____ on Mia.

Down

1. Mum says we're not ____ to go swimming today.
2. Another name for Dad.
5. Sounds like your male parent – but means further away.

Alter this!

Can you tell the difference between these words?

- *altar* – a sort of table that you find in a church
- *alter* – to change something
- *bridal* – to do with a bride
- *bridle* – straps that are used to control a horse.

1. **Correct these sentences by crossing out the wrong words, and writing the correct words above them. The first one has been done for you.**

a. There was a beautiful vase of flowers on the ~~alter~~. *altar*

b. Janine looked lovely in her bridle gown.

c. If only I could go back in time, I would altar the past.

d. Jo put the saddle and bridal on her horse.

e. Sunlight poured through the church window and shone brightly on the alter.

f. The bride held the horse's bridal as she and the groom galloped away.

g. Janine's wedding dress came from a specialist bridle shop.

h. The dressmaker allowed time to altar the gown before the wedding day.

2. **Only one of these sentences has the correct homophone. Tick the box to show which one.**

a. The horse's bridal was too tight. ☐

b. The groom felt very relieved when the bridal car drew up to the church and his wife-to-be got out. ☐

c. I need to altar some of these spellings. ☐

Do you assent?

Here are two more pairs of homophones that can cause trouble:

* *assent* means to agree, or agreement. It can be a noun (for example, *I gave my assent*) or a verb (*I assented to the plan*).
* *ascent* means the act of going up (ascending): *I finally completed the ascent of the mountain.*
* *dissent* means to disagree, or disagreement. It can be a noun: (*I expressed my dissent*) or a verb (*I dissented from the plan*).
* *descent* means the act of going down (descending): *I was looking forward to the descent from the mountain.*

1. Use these words to fill the gaps in the sentences below. You can change the endings of the verbs to fit the sentences if you need to.

a. I enjoyed the _____ to the top of the hill, because the view from the cable car was wonderful.

b. Mum had a difficult _____ down the ladder – she fell and hurt her ankle.

c. I had to _____ from the plan to go for a helicopter ride, because I'm scared of heights.

d. I love Italian food, so I _____ to the idea of getting a pizza for dinner.

e. When the mountaineers started their _____ from the top of the mountain, it was still light.

2. Write a sentence using each of these words correctly.

ascent: _____

assent: _____

descent: _____

dissent: _____

Have you heard?

Look at the words in the boxes below. They are *homophones*, so they sound alike but they have different meanings.

1. Draw lines between the boxes to link the words that are homophones.

herd: a group of animals such as cows

led: past tense of the verb *lead*, such as *Max **led** the way out to the playground.*

mourning: feeling very sad about something

guest: a visitor

guessed: past tense of the verb *guess*, such as *I guessed the right answer to the question.*

morning: the part of the day before noon

heard: past tense of the verb *hear*, such as *Have you heard the news?*

lead: the name of a metal.

2. The homophones have been mixed up in the sentences below. Cross out the wrong words, and write the correct word above them.

a. Grandad often has a guessed to stay.

b. Led is one of the heaviest metals.

c. I herd a heard of cows walking down the country lane.

d. The funeral guessed was morning the death of his friend.

e. It's a beautiful mourning this mourning!

f. Ruby needs to sharpen the led in her pencil.

Homophone search

1. Write the homophone or near-homophone for each of the words below. If you're not sure, look back at pages 33 to 38. The first one has been done for you.

isle _____aisle_____   guessed _____

aloud _____   herd _____

led _____   affect _____

bridle _____   mourning _____

father _____   assent _____

dissent _____

2. Now find the words you have written in the grid below. Search across and down. Circle them as you find them.

a	s	c	e	n	t	i	h	o	c	k	s	s	t
i	p	s	d	e	s	c	e	n	t	m	f	l	o
s	i	r	d	a	f	l	a	l	l	o	w	e	d
l	e	e	m	t	a	g	r	t	u	r	n	a	e
e	g	b	e	b	r	i	d	a	l	n	b	d	f
g	u	e	s	t	i	l	o	m	a	i	r	g	f
f	e	a	g	r	o	o	i	d	e	n	i	u	e
f	a	r	t	h	e	r	l	f	m	g	m	e	c
t	r	g	o	l	a	r	p	e	n	a	l	r	t

3. Choose a homophone pair from the homophones on this page. Write two sentences – one using each word in the pair. Your sentences need to show that you understand what the homophones mean, and can spell them correctly.

_____

_____

Past or passed?

The pairs of words below are easy to mix up.

- *passed* is the past tense of the verb *pass*. For example, *I passed the spelling test easily.*
- *past* has two possible meanings. It can mean the period of time that has already gone by: *In the past, children often had to go out to work.* It can also be a preposition: *I zoomed past Zac and cross the finishing line.*
- *precede* means to go before someone or something. For example, *May precedes June.*
- *proceed* means to go on. For example, *The policeman waved to show the queue of cars could proceed*, or *I proceeded to eat my sandwich.*

1. **Which word above would you be most likely to use if you were describing something that had happened a long time ago?**

_____

2. **Which of these sentences uses the word *precede* correctly?**

a. We had to wait until we had the police officer's permission to precede. ☐

b. I preceded to tell my brother off for being so rude. ☐

c. The summer holiday precedes the start of the new school year. ☐

3. **Circle the correct word or words to use in each of these sentences.**

a. On our walk we **passed** / **past** right **passed** / **past** the school gates.

b. My birthday **precedes** / **proceeds** my Mum's by six days.

c. I'm glad I don't live in the **passed** / **past**, before computers were invented.

d. We **preceded** / **proceeded** with our original plan to go for a picnic.

4. **Write a sentence using each of these words correctly.**

proceed: _____

precede: _____

Cereal confusion

Here are two more pairs of confusing homophones.

* *cereal* means grains, like oats, wheat and barley, or things made from grains, like breakfast cereal.

* *serial* is connected to the word *series*. It means a group of things coming one after another, such as a TV serial.

You might know a joke that uses this pair of homophones: *I could murder a bowl of cornflakes – does that make me a cereal killer?*

* A *compliment* is a nice comment about someone – for example, *I complimented Mrs Turner on her smart new haircut*, or *Gran paid Tom a compliment on his excellent cooking*.

* To *complement* something is to make it complete, or to go well with it – for example, *The red cushions complemented the dark grey sofa perfectly.*

1. Choose the correct words to fill the gaps in these sentences.

a. I usually have a bowl of _____ for breakfast.

b. I _____ Zoe on her hat, which _____ her outfit perfectly.

c. I never miss *Werewolves in Wolverhampton* – it's my favourite _____.

d. Wheat, barley, corn and rice are all _____.

e. Jack got lots of _____ on his goalkeeping skills.

f. Jack's team is good because the players all have skills that _____ each other.

2. Which sentence uses the right homophone?

a. I always feel embarrassed when someone complements me. ☐

b. The dark green of Jade's dress complimented the colour of her eyes. ☐

c. I couldn't believe it when my little brother actually paid me a compliment! ☐

3. Rewrite the two mispelled words in question 2. Cross them out and rewrite above them.

Desert island homophones

Here are some more easily confused words.

- A **des**ert (with the stress on the first syllable, 'des') is a dry place where not many plants and animals live.

- If you des**ert** someone or something (with the stress on the second syllable, 'ert'), you abandon it.

- A dess**ert** (with the stress on the second syllable, 'ert') is a pudding or sweet that you eat after a main meal.

- A draft is a go at writing something – for example, *I threw away the first draft of my letter because of all the spelling mistakes.*

- If you draft someone or something in, you call on them for extra help – for example, *I had to draft in all my friends to help clear up the mess on the pitch.*

- A draught is a gust of air – for example, *There was a cold draught coming from the open window.*

---

1.   Read this diary of a castaway. Fill the gaps with the correct words from the list above.

Dear Diary,

This is my second night on this _____ island. I have been _____

by all my friends, and I am feeling very lonely. I'd feel a bit better if I weren't so hungry! I would

give anything for a delicious sweet _____ like the ones the ship's cook used to

make! I have decided to _____ a letter and put it in a bottle. I will throw it into the

waves and hope someone finds it. If only there were someone else on this island, whom I could

_____ in to help me! But all I can see around me is the _____,

stretching on for miles and miles. Even the ship's dog, Trixie, has _____ me!

As night draws on, it is getting colder. There is a nasty _____ coming through

the cracks in my shelter. Oh well, I'd better get some sleep. Perhaps I'll have better luck

in the morning.

Tommy

Principle or principal?

Even very good spellers sometimes get the words below muddled up.

- *principal* can be an adjective meaning *most important*. For example, *Amy was the principal dancer in the show.*

- *principal* can also be used as a noun meaning a leader or head. For example, *Amy's mum was the principal of the local college.*

- *principle* is a noun meaning a basic truth or belief. For example, *Most people agree with the principle that stealing is wrong.*

- *profit* normally means the money made when you sell something; it can also mean an advantage. For example, *There is no profit in cheating in an exam.*

- a *prophet* is someone who foretells the future.

1. Choose the correct words to fill the gaps in these sentences.

a. Jason made a lot of _____ when he sold his biscuits at the school fair.

b. The _____ of the school, Mrs Andrews, came to congratulate Jason.

c. Mrs Andrews is a firm believer in the _____ that everyone should work together.

d. Being kind and respectful of each other is the _____ rule of the school.

e. I am not a _____, but I predict that with the _____, the school will be able to buy lots of new sports equipment now!

2. Which sentence uses the correct homophone? Tick your choice.

a. My mum always sticks to the principal that we should finish our homework before we watch TV. ☐

b. The principle problem I have with this is that I always miss my favourite programmes. ☐

c. Sometimes my mum's principles can be very inconvenient. ☐

3. Rewrite the two mispelled words in question 2. Cross them out and rewrite above them.

Spelling

Be wary!

1. The words in the boxes below are pairs of homophones or commonly confused words. Draw lines between the boxes to link the pairs of words.

> **stationary:** still, not moving

> **wary:** if you are *wary* about something, you are cautious and alert to possible danger

> **whose:** belonging to someone – for example, *Whose lunchbox is that?*

> **steal:** to take something without permission

> **weary:** tired

> **stationery:** things you use for writing, such as paper and envelopes

> **steel:** a sort of metal

> **who's:** a shorter way of saying *who is* or *who has*

2. The homophones and near-homophones have been mixed up in the sentences below. Cross out the wrong words, and write the correct words above them.

a. I can't work out who's clothes are who's.

b. Whose going to set the table for lunch?

c. Jake was scared of dogs, so he felt rather weary when he heard barking.

d. Allie was very wary after her long walk.

e. Who's stationary set is this?

f. The train was stationery for a long time.

g. I saw Callum steel the biscuits.

Crossophone

1. **The answers to the crossword clues below are all homophones or near-homophones. If you need a hint, look back at pages 33 to 44.**

Across
1. A basic belief.
5. Your dad.
6. Go before.
9. To change something is to a _____ it.
10. I would never have g _____ that you were such a good dancer!
12. A word that means the same as *further*.
14. A very heavy metal.
16. A dry and barren place.
17. All the things you need if you're going to do some writing.

Down
1. We p_____ the school as we walked into town.
2. When someone says something nice about you, it's a _____.
3. Someone who can see into the future.
4. Bad weather often has an _____ on people's plans.
7. When you go down the mountain, you make a _____.
8. Rain may _____ our plan to have a picnic.
9. A word that means the same as *permitted*.
10. A visitor who comes to stay.
11. The money you might make if you sell something.
13. Have you h_____ the latest news?
15. A cold gust of air.

Vocabulary

Story language

The story below includes lots of synonyms (words with similar meanings) – but some of them are too informal, and some of them are too boring.

1. Read the story.
2. Highlight or underline the synonyms that you think are most interesting and appropriate for the story.

Prince Charming was a **good-looking** / **handsome** / **brave** / **charming** young **man** / **guy** / **youth** / **prince**. He heard that a **cute** / **beautiful** / **nice** / **pretty** princess was sleeping in an **ancient** / **old** / **impregnable** / **enormous** castle and could only be woken with a kiss. The problem was that the castle was protected by a **huge** / **prickly** / **thorny** / **big** hedge. The hedge was so **prickly** / **dangerous** / **high** / **perilous** that many knights had died trying to climb over it.

It was a **horrible** / **nasty** / **fearsome** / **scary** sight. The thorns were as big as **daggers** / **kitchen knives** / **dragon's teeth** / **rulers**, and **skeletons** / **corpses** / **dead bodies** / **cadavers** hung from them. The air was filled with the **stench** / **pong** / **smell** / **aroma** of their rotting bodies.

But Prince Charming was not **scared** / **deterred** / **put off** / **frightened**. He walked **bravely** / **courageously** / **determinedly** / **quickly** towards the hedge and, to his amazement, the thorns turned to **beautiful** / **lovely** / **nice** / **pretty** flowers. That was because the 100-year spell ended at that moment – even though the prince knew nothing about it.

He walked **happily** / **eagerly** / **quickly** / **excitedly** to the castle where he found everybody **snoozing** / **sleeping** / **dozing** / **resting**. Then he found his way to Sleeping Beauty's tower. He had never seen anyone so **nice** / **sweet** / **cute** / **lovely**. Her skin was as pale as **milk** / **snow** / **paper** / **silk** and her lips were as red as **blood** / **roses** / **paint** / **lipstick**.

He kissed her and she awoke with a **jerk** / **start** / **twitch** / **jump**.

"What time is it?" she said **quietly** / **breathlessly** / **curiously** / **sleepily**.

"It's five and twenty past eight in the morning of March the first, 1492."

"Oh, dear," she **moaned** / **sighed** / **groaned** / **complained**, "that's much too early." And she went back to sleep for another **2** / **10** / **100** / **1,000,000** years!

Official language

Official forms and documents normally use language in a very precise, formal way. They often use complex sentences, imperative forms of verbs and formal, subject-specific vocabulary.

1. **Read this text, which is an extract from DVLA leaflet D100.**
2. **Underline the complex sentences.**
3. **Draw a wavy line under any sentences that use the imperative (commands).**
4. **Draw a ring round words which are formal or subject-specific.**

Driver and Vehicle Licensing Agency (DVLA)

1. PHOTOCARD DRIVING LICENCES

DVLA now only issues photocard driving licences. This is to improve road safety by eliminating impersonation at driving tests and ensuring the person driving a vehicle is qualified to do so.

You will be issued with:

- a photocard; showing
  - the driver's photograph and signature which is electronically copied from the application form
  - categories of vehicles the driver is entitled to drive
- a paper counterpart document, showing
  - your signature (also electronically copied)
  - details of any endorsements, and in the case of a full licence holder, any provisional driving entitlement held.

Note: You must produce *both* the photocard and counterpart if requested by the police or a court. You should also present both parts when taking a driving test. You may also find that other organisations, such as car hire firms and insurance companies, will ask to see both parts.

Drivers will need to renew their photocard licence every ten years until age 70 to keep the photograph up to date. This will not affect the validity period of the entitlement shown on the licence. DVLA will send a reminder when the photograph is due for renewal. Drivers who are required to renew their licence at shorter intervals, for example, for medical reasons, or because they hold entitlement to drive buses or lorries, will not be required to renew their photograph at each renewal.

Vocabulary

A formal interview

When we talk to friends, we can use language that is very informal. However, some conversations need more formal language. In a *formal interview* we normally use standard English, and try to make our words sound like written language.

1. **Fill in the blanks below to help you plan a formal interview. Remember to write your questions in whole sentences, using formal words and standard English. Extra idea: Ask a partner to be your interviewee. Can they reply to your questions using formal standard English?**

Name of interviewer: _____ Name of guest: _____

a. Open the interview and greet your guest.

_____

b. Begin with a question about their family background.

_____

c. Then ask a question about friendships.

_____

d. Ask a question about hobbies and leisure activities.

_____

e. Ask a question about academic likes and dislikes.

_____

f. Ask a question about future goals and ambitions.

_____

g. Add a question of your own choice, based on your knowledge of the guest.

_____

h. End the interview appropriately.

_____

A formal letter

If you are writing a letter to someone you don't know – for example, to make a complaint or ask for help – you need to use formal language.

Here is one occasion when a formal letter is appropriate:

Luke Jones bought a computer game, but when he tried to load it, the message 'Insufficient data' appeared on his screen. He followed all the instructions, but it still didn't work. He went back to the shop, but the assistant first ignored him, and then refused to give him an exchange or a refund.

1. Read this letter, which Luke wrote to the shop manager.

To the manager,

I got a game from your shop on Saturday when me and my mum was shopping. When I got it home, I stuck it in my computer, but it wouldn't load. I was unhappy. My mum said to take it back to the shop. I came back to the shop and a different guy was on the till. He told me the game was OK and it must be the way I was loading it. I felt bad as my mum wasn't with me and I didn't know what to say.

When I got home my mum said I should write down my complaint, so I am. Please write back to me.

From
Luke Jones, aged 10

2. Rewrite Luke's letter, using more formal language.

Literal and figurative language

Literal	Figurative	
	Simile	**Metaphor**
Straightforward, factual way of saying something	A comparison using *like* or *as*	A direct comparison saying one thing is another
My feet are cold. Ordinary post is slow. He is tall.	My feet are like ice. Ordinary post is as slow as a snail. He is as tall as a giant.	My feet are ice. Ordinary post is snail mail. He is a giant of a man.
Own examples		

Introducing expanded noun phrases

Expanded noun phrases are a way of adding more information about a noun. Sometimes we use nouns in sentences without a lot of extra detail, for example:

- *My friend came round yesterday.*
  In this sentence, *My friend* is a noun phrase. It takes the noun *friend* and gives us a little bit of extra information – it's not just any old friend, it's *my* friend.

However, sometimes you might want to add more detail than this – and that's when expanded noun phrases come in handy. Here's the same sentence with an expanded noun phrase:

- *My best friend, Tom, came round yesterday.*
  We now know a lot more about the friend – it's my best friend, and his name is Tom.
  You can expand a noun phrase even more than this. Look at this example:
- *My zany, football-loving best friend, Tom, came round yesterday.*

---

1. **The noun phrases are underlined in the sentences below. Write the sentences out again, but this time add some extra description or detail to create expanded noun phrases like the examples above. The first one has been done for you.**

a. <u>My brother</u> was crying.

  Expanded version: My sulky little brother was crying.

b. <u>The dog</u> was barking.

  Expanded version: _____

c. <u>A dragon</u> flew overhead.

  Expanded version: _____

d. Tom put on <u>his football boots</u>.

  Expanded version: _____

e. I sat on <u>the chair</u>.

  Expanded version: _____

f. I like <u>spaghetti</u>.

  Expanded version: _____

More expanded noun phrases

In the expanded noun phrases on page 51, most of the extra words have been added *before* the noun. For example, in *My sulky little brother*, the noun *brother* comes at the end of the phrase. You can add extra words *after* the noun in a noun phrase, too. Here are some examples, with the noun phrases underlined:

- *Ella gasped when she saw <u>the mansion</u>.*
- *Ella gasped when she saw <u>the deserted, spooky old mansion perched on the high clifftop</u>.*
- *We had our picnic by <u>a stream</u>.*
- *We had our picnic by a <u>delightful, clear stream, with tiny fish darting here and there</u>.*

All of the extra words in the expanded versions add more information about the main nouns, *mansion* and *stream*.

1. Add some more words before and after the nouns in the sentences below, to create expanded noun phrases.

a. James was amazed to see <u>the giant</u>.

Expanded version: _____

b. I was cold, so I put on <u>my jumper</u>.

Expanded version: _____

2. Underline the expanded noun phrases in the sentences below. The first one has been done for you.

a. I puffed and panted as I climbed up to <u>the ancient, crumbling ruin at the top of the hill</u>.

b. The energetic young girl, with her long, curly hair flying behind her, ran down the hill.

c. The striker scored an amazing goal which flew like a bird into the back of the net.

d. Alice stepped into a well-tended garden full of blossoming flowers and trees.

e. I like nothing better than a large, steaming cup of delicious hot chocolate with cream and marshmallows on top.

f. Dad's ancient car, with its missing wing-mirror and broken door, jerked and jolted into view.

Expand it!

1. **Choose some words from the box below to help you expand these noun phrases. You can add your own words too. Remember to choose words that will really help your reader to imagine the thing you are describing.**

kind * furious * intense * young * serene * delighted * peaceful
toothy * starlit * dependable * reassuring * old * deserted

the doctor
Your expanded noun phrase:

_____

the scene
Your expanded noun phrase:

_____

a frown
Your expanded noun phrase:

_____

2. **Expand these noun phrases by adding words to fill the blanks. You can add more than one word in each space if you like.**

A _____, _____ glass of _____ milk.

A _____, _____ scarf that _____

_____

My _____ game that _____

_____

A _____, _____ rabbit with _____

_____

Info-packed phrases

Expanded noun phrases can help writers give lots of information in a quick and concise way. Look at this example:

- *My sister Margo is eight. She can play the piano, and she loves spending time on the computer. She is in hospital at the moment. She has appendicitis.*
- *My piano-playing, eight-year-old sister Margo, who is a computer whizz, is in hospital with appendicitis.*

The underlined words are an expanded noun phrase. All of the information in the first two sentences of the original example is packed into this phrase.

1. Underline the expanded noun phrases in the examples below.

a. The exhausted, red-faced runner, who had been running for three hours, finally crossed the finish line.

b. A silent, cunning fox, with moonlight glinting in his eyes, crept slowly towards the ramshackle old hen house.

c. The three clever, sprightly goats outwitted the huge, warty troll under the bridge.

d. The forbidding castle, with its tall towers covered in ivy, loomed into view out of the dark, swirling mist.

2. Turn each group of short sentences into one sentence, including an expanded noun phrase.

a. When I got home I found something waiting for me. It was totally unexpected! It was a present. It lay on the end of my bed. It was beautifully wrapped.

_____

b. A gnome was shouting at me. It was tiny! It was very cross. It was dressed all in green.

_____

c. My dog's name is Digger. He is as quick as lightning. He loves to chase balls. He went racing across the field.

_____

Slick descriptions

1. **Write a sentence about each of the people shown in the pictures, using expanded noun phrases. The first one has been done for you.**

optician

The kind and friendly optician, who liked to put people at their ease, examined the boy's eyes with her instruments.

politician

_____

_____

musician

_____

_____

scientist

_____

_____

magician

_____

_____

2. **Look back at the sentences you have written and circle the expanded noun phrases.**

Using the perfect form of verbs

We use the *perfect form* of verbs when we want to talk or write about something that has already happened in the past. Here's an example of the *present perfect* form:
- *I have eaten all the cake.*

You can tell that this sentence is in the present perfect, because the helping verb *have* is in the present tense, but the main verb *eaten* is in the past tense. The sentence is set in the present, but it tells us about something that has already happened.

Here's an example of the *past perfect* form:
- *Mum **had left** the cake out on the table.*

You can tell that this is in the past perfect, because the helping verb *had* is in the past tense, and so is the main verb *left*. So this sentence is talking about something that had already happened at some point in the past.

1. Write *present perfect* or *past perfect* next to each of the sentences below.

a. I had never seen such an enormous dog._____.

b. Gran has made a delicious chicken pie for tea. _____.

c. After I had opened my birthday presents, I gave everyone a thank-you hug. _____.

d. I have always wanted a pet iguana. _____.

e. Mum had put the biscuits on a very high shelf. _____.

2. Rewrite the sentences below so that they use the past perfect form.

a. I have spent all morning tidying my bedroom.

_____

b. Sam looked everywhere for his pen.

_____

c. Ellie has gone to the shops to get some sweets.

_____

When and why?

We often use the perfect form of verbs when we want to explain when or why something happened. Look at these examples:

* *After I had finished my bath, I got into my cosy, warm pyjamas.*
Here, the past perfect form *had finished* helps to tell us the order things happened in – first I had my bath, then I got into my pyjamas.

* *Jamila is happy, because she has finished doing her homework.*
Here, the present perfect form *has finished* helps to tell us why Jamila is happy – it's because she has already finished her homework at the time we are talking about.

1. **Look at these sentences. Write *time* if the past perfect form helps to tell us *when* something happened, and *cause* if it helps to tell us *why* something happened.**

a. As soon as I had taken my coat off, I heard my phone ringing. _____

b. I knew that Ben must be tired, since he had been working very hard. _____

c. Because Mrs Groom had seen Tom pinching Ahmed, she was very angry. _____

d. I zoomed to the park on my bike when I had finished helping Mum tidy up. _____

2. **Re-read the sentences in question 1, and underline the perfect forms of verbs in each sentence.**

3. **Rewrite the sentences below so that they use the perfect form of verbs. The first one has been done for you.**

I finished my tea and then I went round to my friend's house.
When I had finished my tea, I went round to my friend's house.

Jamal played football and then he went home on his bike.

_____

Alina was very hungry because of missing lunch.

_____

Zac's alarm clock didn't go off, and as a result he got to school late.

_____

Grammar

How likely is it?

There is a handy set of verbs called *modal verbs*, which we can use to show how likely something is to happen. All of the following are modal verbs:
will, would, can, could, may, might, shall, should, must, ought

These verbs express different degrees of likelihood. For example:
I will go to the park after school.
is a lot more definite than
I may go to the park after school.

---

1. Underline the modal verbs in these sentences. Watch out: some sentences have two modal verbs.

A troll can eat a whole goat in one go.

The troll will eat the biggest goat first.

The goat would get away if he could.

He should run away as fast as possible.

However, he may have a plan to outwit the troll.

The goat might be lucky, because trolls can be very stupid.

Someone ought to warn the goat that he must be very careful.

We shall see what happens when the goat goes strolling over the troll's bridge.

---

2. Fill the gaps in these sentences with a modal verb. Sometimes there is only one modal verb that fits – other times, you can pick from two or more possible verbs.

Maybe, in the future, people _____ be able to go to the Moon on holiday.

I _____ like to visit the Moon one day.

I _____ start saving my money so I _____ afford a trip to the Moon

one day.

Mum says this is a silly idea and I _____ forget all about it.

I don't think Mum _____ ever get to the Moon.

3. **Look at the modal verbs below. Put all the modal verbs that suggest something will *definitely* happen into one box, and all the modal verbs that suggest something *might* happen into the other box.**

will * would * can * could * may * might * shall * should * must * ought

Definitely	Possibly

4. **Rewrite the sentences below, choosing a different modal verb so that the meaning changes from *definitely* to *possibly*.**

a. I must finish reading this book.

_____

b. Jamie will win the egg and spoon race.

_____

c. We shall go to Blackpool this summer.

_____

d. I will tell you the secret of my success.

_____

5. **Now choose a different modal verb to change these sentences from *possibly* to *definitely*.**

a. I might go round to Tom's house after school.

_____

b. We ought to go and visit Gran.

_____

c. Dan and Ella may win the dance competition again.

_____

d. We could get fish and chips for tea.

_____

Grammar

As well as modal verbs, there are *adverbs* that we can use when we want to write about how likely things are. For example:

probably, surely, maybe, definitely, perhaps, possibly, certainly.

6. **Put the adverbs above in these two boxes, to show how definite they are.**

Definite	Possible

7. **Rewrite the sentences below, adding an adverb to make them sound more likely. The first one has been done for you.**

a. I can go to judo next week.

I can definitely go to judo next week.

b. Jamie will finish the maths test first.

_____

c. We shall enjoy the film.

_____

d. I will remember my Mum's birthday.

_____

8. **Rewrite the sentences below, adding an adverb and changing the modal verbs to make them sound *less* likely. The first one has been done for you.**

a. I will do my homework before bedtime.

I may possibly do my homework before bedtime.

b. My gran can beat your gran at arm-wrestling.

_____

c. Our pet rabbit, Coco, will escape from the hutch.

_____

All in a good clause

Relative clauses give more information about nouns. They are usually introduced by a relative pronoun – for example:
who, which, whose, where, when, that.

1. Choose a relative pronoun from the list above to introduce the relative clauses below. The first one has been done for you.

Noun (in bold)	Relative pronoun	Relative clause
This is the **programme**	that	I told you about.
Cabot is the **explorer**		discovered Newfoundland.
I wish to see the **boy**		football boots were left in the classroom.
Please upgrade the **computers**		are in the computer room.
I enjoyed the **day**		I won the race.
This is for the **girl**		lost her history book.
Here is the **canteen**		we eat lunch.
The telescope is an **instrument**		makes it possible to see distant planets.
I first saw the **girl**		she was playing tennis.
Kari was a new **pupil**		childhood had been spent in Kosovo.
Iceland is a **country**		is north of Scotland.
This is the **street**		my gran lives.

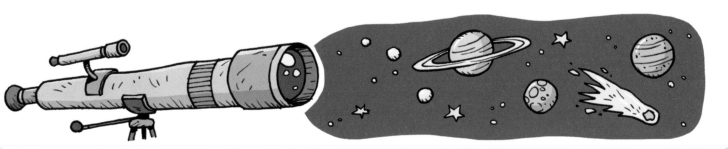

Grammar

2. **The wrong relative pronouns have been used in the sentences below. Cross out the pronouns that are wrong, and write the correct pronouns. The first one has been done for you.**

who * which * whose * where * when * that

a. On the wall was a portrait ~~who~~ **which** was beautifully painted.

b. I was ill on the day where we learned about long division.

c. I've finished the homework who Mrs Gibson gave us.

d. Daniel ran after his hat where was blown away by a strong wind.

e. This is the dragon which treasure was stolen by the dwarves.

f. I have a computer when is very old and slow.

g. I always like revisiting the places who we went when I was little.

h. Lucy is the girl which books went missing.

i. My favourite TV programmes are the ones who are funny.

j. I was very happy the year which we moved to London.

k. Mr Prendergast shouted at the boy that ball broke his window.

l. I patted my new puppy, whose was very excited.

It's all relative

As well as adding more information about a noun, you can also use relative clauses to add more information about another clause. Here's an example:
We took a long time to walk home, which meant we missed tea.
Here, the *which* refers back to the whole of the first clause in the sentence, *We took a long time to walk home.*

1.   Draw lines to link the two halves of the sentences below. All of the sentences include a relative pronoun.

Dad suddenly realised he was wearing odd socks,

Janie walked down the street

Greg is the boy

I ate the sandwich

The mouse disappeared into a tiny hole,

My favourite city is Dublin,

Mrs Baxter introduced the girl

I was getting out of the shower at the very moment

This is the famous athlete

I was ill on Wednesday,

which has many beautiful buildings.

which Mum had made for me.

when you knocked at the door.

where the famous actor lived.

which he found very embarrassing.

whose shoes got lost.

which meant I missed the play.

who won the marathon.

which annoyed the cat.

who was coming to join our class.

Grammar

Sometimes, the relative pronoun *that* is left out of a relative clause. We don't need to include it because it can be worked out, or implied, from the rest of the sentence. For example, you could say:
*This is the car **that** I saw outside your house.*
Or you could say:
This is the car I saw outside your house.
These two sentences mean exactly the same thing.

2. **Draw lines to link the two halves of the sentences below. They all use relative clauses where the word *that* has been left out.**

The donkey

This is the road

Have you seen the book

Did you spot the cake

The cat

I hid inside the cupboard?

I put down on the table?

I always walk down on the way to school.

we saw in the garden was ginger.

I rode was very bad-tempered.

3. **Cross out the pronouns that are wrong in these sentences, and write the correct pronouns.**

a. Have you got a spare pencil who you don't need?

b. I walked across the grassy field whose the dogs were playing happily.

c. Mahmoud and Alex were fighting again, when annoyed Mrs James.

d. It was my birthday on the day which the great flood started.

e. I saw the tiny purple aliens when zoomed across the sky.

f. Elephants have long trunks who they can use to pick things up.

g. Daisy is the girl which helped Mr Moore to tidy up.

h. School is closed today, when is the reason why I am at home.

'Verbing' nouns and adjectives

You can turn some nouns and adjectives into verbs by adding the suffixes **'ate'**, **'ise'** and **'ify'**. Sometimes you have to take off another suffix or change the root word a bit first. Here are some examples:

noun: *accommodation*	+ **'ate'**	= verb: *accommodate*
adjective: *active*	+ **'ate'**	= verb: *activate*
adjective: *authentic*	+ **'ate'**	= verb: *authenticate*
noun: *stimulus*	+ **'ate'**	= verb: *stimulate*
noun: *apology*	+ **'ise'**	= verb: *apologise*
noun: *demon*	+ **'ise'**	= verb: *demonise*
noun: *drama*	+ **'ise'**	= verb: *dramatise*
noun: *beauty*	+ **'ify'**	= verb: *beautify*
noun: *electricity*	+ **'ify'**	= verb: *electrify*
noun: *purity*	+ **'ify'**	= verb: *purify*

1. **Add suffixes to the words below to make new words. Write a short definition for each new word you make.**

reunite + 'ify' = _____

category + 'ise' = _____

solid + 'ify' = _____

facility + 'ate' = _____

advert + 'ise' = _____

origin + 'ate' = _____

_____

_____

_____

_____

_____

_____

Grammar

2. Process the nouns and adjectives through the suffix box to make new *real* words. Adapt the stem if necessary and write the new words.

Nouns and adjectives:

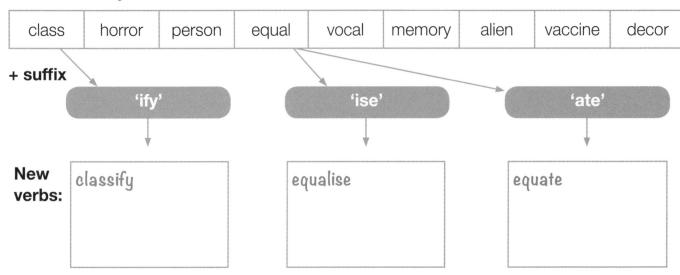

| class | horror | person | equal | vocal | memory | alien | vaccine | decor |

+ suffix

'ify'　　　　'ise'　　　　'ate'

New verbs:

classify　　　　equalise　　　　equate

---

3. Write definitions for these verbs.

a. *classify* means _____

b. *equalise* means _____

c. *equate* means _____

---

4. The Word Police are looking for an escaped noun. He is hiding among these verbs. When you spot him, put a ring round him. See if you can capture him in a sentence with one of the verbs. Write the sentence below.

evaluate * generate * speculate * truncate * vaccinate
retaliate * translate * gyrate * rotate * pirate * agitate * liberate
nominate * anticipate * celebrate * elevate * motivate

_____

_____

_____

Verbs and their opposites

You can change the meaning of some verbs – or even change them into their opposite – by adding a prefix. It's a bit like being a magician: you can make verbs *appear and **dis**appear.* You have to be careful, though – you can't do this with every verb. The main prefixes which can be used to change the meaning of a verb into its opposite are **'dis'**, **'de'** and **'mis'**.

1. **Look at the verbs below. Add one of the prefixes above to each verb, to change the meaning. Remember: It needs to make a real word.**

connect + dis = disconnect

behave + _____ = _____

approve + _____ = _____

hear + _____ = _____

clutter + _____ = _____

understand + _____ = _____

like + _____ = _____

throne + _____ = _____

obey + _____ = _____

mystify + _____ = _____

2. **Add a prefix to the verbs in these sentences so that the sentences change their meaning.**

a. The soldiers _____activated the mines that had been buried in the ground.

b. My teacher, Mrs Turner, _____approves of people who give in their homework late.

c. The letter never reached my cousin because I _____addressed the envelope.

d. I _____believed my brother when he said he had seen a pixie in our garden.

e. We _____trusted the enemy when they told us they wanted to surrender.

More verb prefixes

Prefixes help you to change the meaning of verbs in lots of ways – they don't just turn verbs into their opposites, as on page 67. These are all verb prefixes:
'over', **'re'**, **'pre'** and **'under'**.

---

1.   Add the prefix 'over' to the verbs below. Then write a short definition.

a.   over + sleep = oversleep   **Definition**: sleeping for too long

b.   over + work = _____   _____

c.   over + act = _____   _____

---

2.   Now add the prefix 're' to these verbs, and write a definition.

a.   re + visit = revisit   **Definition**: to visit it again

b.   re + build = _____   _____

c.   re + activate = _____   _____

---

3.   Try the same with the verbs below, using the prefix 'pre'.

a.   pre + dispose = predispose   **Definition**: to make someone more likely to do something

b.   pre + judge = _____   _____

c.   pre + amble = _____   _____

---

4.   And now do the same thing with these verbs, using the prefix 'under'.

a.   under + sea = undersea   **Definition**: below the sea or ocean

b.   under + value = _____   _____

c.   under + achieve = _____   _____

Making links

There are lots of words that we can use to help us make links within and between sentences and paragraphs.

For example, we can use *adverbs* and *adverbials* like these:

then, after, that, this, firstly, later, nearby, unfortunately, just then.

We can also use *conjunctions* like these:

although, and, as, because, but, for, until, when, where, while.

Words like these help us to link different ideas in our writing. For example, look at these sentences:

Firstly*, I added four tablespoons of salt to the water.* **Then** *I stirred it* **until** *the salt dissolved* **and** *the liquid was clear. Five minutes* **later** *I heated the liquid to boiling point.*

The words in bold help to show the order in which the actions were done, and how the actions connect to each other. Making links like this is sometimes described as **building cohesion**. The underlined words all help to make *cohesive links* within and between the sentences.

1. Underline the words and phrases that help to build cohesion in the paragraphs below.

Because I was very hungry, I decided to make myself a sandwich. Firstly, I took two slices of bread, and then I went to the fridge because I wanted to get some cheese. However, there was no cheese in the fridge, so I had to use peanut butter instead.

When I had finally found the peanut butter, I spread it thickly on one of the slices of bread. Then I put the other slice of bread on top. Next, I cut the sandwich into four triangles. I always cut my sandwiches like this. When I had put the sandwich on my favourite plate, I sat down at the table to eat it.

Unfortunately, just at that moment, my sister came running into the room. "Great!" she said. "You've made me a sandwich!"

Before I could say a word, she grabbed my sandwich and started to eat it. I tried to stop her, but it was too late. She wolfed that sandwich down, and then asked for more.

Grammar

2. Read the information text below. Lots of the words and phrases that help to create cohesion have been left out. Write them back in again. Sometimes there is more than one word or phrase you could use – you can choose which you think sounds best. Look back at page 69 if you need a reminder about words and phrases that create cohesion.

The platypus is a most unusual kind of mammal. _____ other mammals give birth to live young, the female platypus lays two soft-shelled eggs _____ she incubates for one to two weeks. _____ the eggs hatch, she feeds the young with milk from her milk glands. The young do not suck on the milk glands. Instead, they _____ push at the glands and _____ suck the milk which oozes out into their mother's fur. Another interesting feature of the platypus is its large, soft beak or bill. It _____ is so sensitive it is able to detect the small creatures in the water _____ the platypus feeds upon. Its sensitive beak is invaluable, _____ the platypus is blind _____ deaf when it is in the water. The platypus has a furry body, _____ four legs with webbed feet. It uses its front legs to paddle _____ its hind legs to swim, enabling it to swim strongly under the water. Male platypuses have a poison gland on their ankles _____ they use to fend off enemies. Adult platypuses weigh up to 2.4kg, _____ males grow up to 60cm _____ females are slightly smaller. Platypuses are found only in parts of Australia and Tasmania.

Combine sentences

1. **Combine sentences by adding the appropriate conjunctions in the empty box. Look for more than one possible conjunction.**

although * and * as * because * but * for * until * when * where * while

The girls were frightened		they heard the thunder.
They got soaked		it rained unexpectedly.
They decided to take shelter		the rain stopped.
Tara felt uneasy		they entered the old house.
Zara tried to switch on the lights		there was no electricity.
Tara opened a cupboard		she found a skeleton.
She was about to scream		Zara pointed out that it was plastic.
The girls tried to sleep		they were too nervous.
Zara woke up early		a cock crowed loudly.
Tara was happy		the rain had stopped.

The Arctic and the Antarctic

1.   Look at the information below.

Same	Different
• long, dark freezing nights • no light in winter • icebergs are a common sight • affected by pollution • scientific stations present • minerals discovered • home to a large number of fish • regions are overfished.	• Arctic is in the north; Antarctic is in the south • Arctic centre is a frozen sea; Antarctic is frozen land • Antarctic is colder • Arctic has polar bears; Antarctic has penguins • Antarctic is now a world park • Minerals mined in Arctic.

2.   Write two paragraphs, one describing the Arctic and one describing the Antarctic, based on the information given above. Don't forget to add words and phrases to build cohesion – look back at page 69 for a reminder.

The Arctic _____

_____

_____

_____

_____

The Antarctic _____

_____

_____

_____

_____

_____

Zoos

A class of children have brainstormed about the need for zoos.

Zoos have saved many animals from extinction.

Zoos are unfair to animals.

Zoos allow people to see animals they would never see otherwise.

The animals change in captivity – sometimes they become neurotic.

They confine animals in small spaces.

Zoos don't give the animals a natural life.

It means people can observe them and learn about them.

The animals have a safer life in the zoo than in the wild.

They provide entertainment for people.

Zoos cost too much and people can't afford to go to them.

It means more people are interested in the animals.

People can see these animals living in the wild on the television; they don't need to go to a zoo.

---

1.   Sort their arguments into two columns, under the headings *For* and *Against*.

For: _____   Against: _____

_____   _____

_____   _____

_____   _____

_____   _____

_____   _____

_____   _____

2. Use the arguments you listed on page 73 to help you write two paragraphs in favour of zoos, and two paragraphs against zoos. Don't forget to use words and phrases to build cohesion within and between your paragraphs – look back at page 69 if you need a reminder about this.

In favour of zoos _____

_____

_____

_____

_____

_____

_____

_____

Against zoos: _____

_____

_____

_____

_____

_____

_____

_____

Crystal clear commas

There are lots of reasons why commas are useful. Here are a couple of reasons that you probably already know:

- They help to separate items in a list.

- They can help to make a longer or more complex sentence, like this one, easier to read.

Commas can also help to make information clearer. For example, these two sentences mean different things, but the only difference between them is the commas:

All the children who handed in their homework late are in trouble with Mr Marsh.
All the children, who handed in their homework late, are in trouble with Mr Marsh.

The first sentence means that Mr Marsh is cross with those children who handed in their homework late – there might be other children with whom Mr Marsh is not cross.
The second sentence means that Mr Marsh is cross with **all** the children, and they **all** handed in their homework late. The commas are needed to make this clear!

1. Add commas to make the meanings of these sentences clearer.

a. The dogs who had rolled about in the mud were given baths.
(Add commas so that you can tell that all the dogs were given baths.)

b. Grandmas who like playing with their grandchildren have lots of fun.
(Add commas so that you can tell the sentence is about all grandmas.)

c. The boys who broke the window were told off.
(Add commas so that the sentence is about all the boys.)

d. The flowers which were my mum's pride and joy got squashed.
(Add commas so that you can tell that all the flowers got squashed.)

2. Add or cross out commas in these sentences so that the meaning changes.

a. I finished my cake sadly.

b. Let's eat, James!

c. Don't, stop!

d. As I was eating the table collapsed.

e. While Mum was cooking the baby started crying.

Punctuation

3. **Rewrite these sentences, adding the missing commas. Look back at page 75 for some examples to help you**

a. The soldiers who had been injured in battle were taken to the hospital.

_____

b. Trombones which make a very loud noise have been banned from the school orchestra.

_____

c. The runners who were on the uphill stretch of the race were puffed out.

_____

d. My favourite breakfast which consists of cornflakes toast orange juice and porridge was waiting for me when I came downstairs.

_____

_____

e. The teachers who are often annoyed with me were waiting for me to come in after lunch.

_____

f. On my birthday which comes just before Christmas I received a new computer game a pair of headphones a book and two pairs of socks as presents.

_____

_____

g. The sharks which had injured fins swam slowly round and round.

_____

h. Outside the shops which are currently closed for refurbishment I met Jamie Alisha and Ben.

_____

Adding commas

1. All the commas have been left out of this piece of text. Can you put them back in?

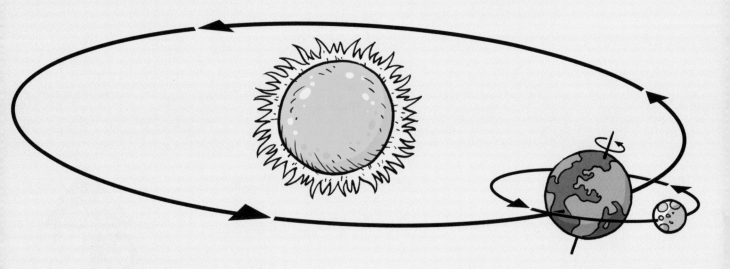

The Sun is at the centre of our Solar System and it is orbited by nine main planets and their satellites. From Earth the Sun and our Moon appear to be the same size but the Sun is approximately 400 times bigger in diameter than the Moon and nearly 400 times further away.

Every day the Sun appears to rise in the east and set in the west but in fact the Sun does not move in this way. Earth rotates on its axis once every 24 hours creating day and night. The rays of light travel from the Sun in straight lines providing us with energy in the form of heat and light.

Although the Moon appears to shine it is not a light source. It actually reflects light from the Sun. The amount of light reflected by the Moon varies depending upon the position of the Moon in relation to the Sun and the Earth. From Earth the Moon appears to change shape depending upon how much light it reflects. We see either a full moon gibbous moon half-moon crescent moon or a new moon.

Sometimes the Sun Earth and Moon line up exactly so that the Moon casts a shadow on the Earth. This is known as a solar eclipse.

Punctuating Rapunzel

Commas are used like brackets to mark off extra information inserted into a sentence. For example:

- sentence: *Rapunzel lived in a tower.*

- sentence + extra information: *Rapunzel, a girl with very long hair, lived in a tower.*

1. Read these sentences. For each one, find the additional information and place a comma before and after it.

The tower a tall building without any steps was Rapunzel's home.

An old woman to whom the tower belonged kept her prisoner.

She would shout her voice croaking cruelly "Rapunzel, let down your hair!"

Rapunzel's hair like a long ladder hung down from the window.

The old woman who was more agile than she looked scrambled up Rapunzel's hair.

A handsome prince who was hiding nearby saw everything that happened.

2. Write three more sentences about Rapunzel, each with correctly punctuated additional information.

_____

_____

_____

_____

_____

Perfect parentheses

A *parenthesis* is a word or phrase which has been added to a sentence, a bit like an afterthought. One way of telling whether a word or phrase is a parenthesis is to try taking it out of the sentence. If the rest of the sentence still makes sense, then you know that the words you removed are a parenthesis.

Here are some sentences where the parenthesis has been underlined. If you read the sentence without the parenthesis, it still makes sense.
The elephants, which had been working all day, were getting tired and hungry.
My friend Cara (who lives next door) has red hair.
The pirates – beards bristling and eyes flashing – boarded the unsuspecting merchant ship.

As you can see from these examples, parentheses normally have punctuation before and after them, to mark them out from the rest of the sentence. There are three different types of punctuation you can use with parentheses: commas, brackets and dashes.

- We use **commas** when the idea in the parenthesis is really an important part of the sentence – it's not a separate idea, it just adds extra information to the sentence.

- We use **brackets** when the idea in the parenthesis isn't really essential to the meaning of the sentence – it's quite useful or interesting, but you could easily leave it out.

- We use **dashes** when we really want to draw attention to the parenthesis. We normally only use dashes when the idea in the parenthesis is unusual, funny or startling in some way.

1. Add the best sort of punctuation to use around the parentheses in these sentences.

a. The ducks swimming serenely on the pond were suddenly disturbed by a loud noise.

b. My uncle Sam whose middle name is Albert loves karaoke.

c. The Second World War which took place between 1939 and 1945 was a time of great hardship for many people.

d. I was sitting quietly in the kitchen when suddenly crash bang wallop I heard a terrible noise from overhead.

e. I love Saturdays which always seem to take forever to come because that is the day when I go to see Gran and Grandpa.

f. Suddenly the door was flung open knocking my little sister flying and a huge giant shouldered his way into the room.

2. Underline the parentheses in the sentences below. Then write each sentence out again, adding commas, brackets or dashes around the parenthesis. Look back at page 79 for a reminder about which sort of punctuation to use when!

Malcolm rushed sweating up to the bus stop.

_____

Just then the bus which had already been waiting several minutes pulled away.

_____

Malcolm who was on his way to an important meeting was very disappointed.

_____

At that moment coming round the corner he saw his friend Priscilla.

_____

Priscilla who worked as a mechanic was driving a brand-new sports car.

_____

The car honking and hooting like crazy drew up by the bus stop.

_____

Malcolm thanking his lucky stars climbed into the passenger seat.

_____

Priscilla who was a very fast driver got Malcolm to his meeting on time.

_____

Phantom phrases

1. **Fill each gap in the passage below with one of the following parentheses. Add a comma before and after the parentheses (unless it comes at the end of a sentence).**

a horrifying creature in a white mask	who was a young chorus girl	in a trembling voice	no matter what other work she had to do	little knowing the price she would pay
if you cooperate with me	on the opening night of the new production	turning white as a sheet	which was a huge building	running backwards and forwards in a panic

The Paris Opera House _____ was said to be

haunted. The ghost _____ had once been a

famous tenor. One day Christine _____ was

sitting alone in her dressing room when she heard a strange voice.

"Christine," whispered the voice, "I can make you famous _____."

"Why do you want to?" answered Christine _____.

"Revenge on Carlotta!" replied the phantom.

From that day onwards _____ the phantom

made Christine practise for at least three hours _____.

Then _____ Carlotta received a threatening note

from the phantom. She read it and _____ fainted.

"Quick!" shouted the manager_____.

"Find Christine. Tell her to put on Carlotta's dress and go on stage!"

So Christine got her chance at last.

Twisted lists

This punctuation mark **:** is called a *colon*. One of the main ways we use colons is to introduce a list. Here are a couple of examples:

I got some unusual presents for my birthday: a flying alien, a pet lizard and a bag of toffees.
Four of my best friends came to help me try out the flying alien: Ashley, Meena, Zac and Jake.

Watch out, though – you don't always need a colon before a list. You only use a colon when the clause before it makes complete sense on its own. *I got some unusual presents for my birthday* makes sense on its own, so we use a colon.
We wouldn't use a colon to introduce this list:
At my birthday party we ate pizza, crisps, grapes and cake.
That's because *At my birthday party we ate* doesn't make sense on its own.

1. **Add punctuation to these lists. Some of them need colons, but not all of them. They all need commas and full stops.**

a. The wizard threw a lot of disgusting things into the cauldron snakes' tongues grasshoppers' legs mud and rotten tomatoes

b. My favourite hobbies are football street dance trampolining and sleeping

c. There are a lot of children in my family four brothers two sisters and fourteen cousins

d. There was a long queue ahead of us at the vet's three cats two dogs a rabbit and four guinea pigs

2. **Turn these clauses into lists starting with colons. You can make up what goes in each list. The first one has been done for you.**

a. I used all these things to make a model robot: an old cereal box, a roller skate, an egg box and my mum's sunglasses.

b. There are lots of places in the world that I would like to visit _____

   _____

c. Under my bed I found some unexpected things _____

d. I made a delicious drink out of all my favourite fruits _____

Helpful hyphens

We use *hyphens* when we want to join two words (or parts of words) together.
One of the main reasons for using a hyphen is to avoid ambiguity. There is a big difference between the meanings of these two phrases, even though they use exactly the same words:

- *a man-eating lion*
- *a man eating lion*

The first one is a dangerous wild beast. The second one is a man with a strange taste in food! So, if you want to make sure that your meaning is clear and not ambiguous, you sometimes need to use a hyphen.

1. Add the missing hyphen to each sentence to make the meaning clear.

a. Around 100 odd people went to the school concert.

b. Jamie's dad is a used car salesman.

c. Al Capone was a well known gangster.

d. In winter I like to wear a fleece lined coat.

e. The top earning film this year was *Delilah Duck's Day Out.*

f. The band One Convention released this year's best selling album.

g. I found a half eaten chocolate bar at the bottom of my bag.

2. Explain the difference between these pairs of phrases. The first one has been done for you.

best selling toy and *best-selling toy:* 'Best selling toy' could mean the best toy that does some selling. 'Best-selling toy' means the toy that sells the best.

second hand clothing and *second-hand clothing:* _____

_____

two month old kittens and *two-month-old kittens:* _____

_____

a half cooked meal and *a half-cooked meal:* _____

_____

Bullet points

Bullet points are very useful when you want to make sure that important information stands out clearly. The way to punctuate bullet points depends on how they are worded.

Some bullet points consist of a whole grammatical sentence, like these.
Here are some of the activities we will do at my party:

- *We will throw wet sponges at my dad.*

- *We will eat pizza.*

- *We will climb on the climbing wall.*

You can see that these bullet points are all punctuated like proper sentences, with capital letters and full stops.
Sometimes, bullet points do not consist of a whole grammatical sentence.
At my party we will:

- *throw wet sponges at my dad*

- *eat pizza*

- *climb on the climbing wall.*

It's a good idea to put a full stop at the end of the last bullet point, to show it's the end of the list. Some people like to use a comma (or even a semicolon) at the end of each bullet point in this kind of list, but that is not essential.
The main rule when punctuating bullet points is – be consistent. Make sure the whole list is punctuated in the same way.

---

1.   Add punctuation and capital letters where necessary to the following bullet point lists.

here are some rules for looking after your pet rabbits

- give them space to hop about freely

- make sure they have plenty of fresh water

- offer them lots of green, leafy vegetables

equipment you might need for your rabbits includes

- bowls for food and water

- a hutch

- a brush, if your rabbits have long fur

When you use bullet points, use a colon to introduce the start of the list. If the bullet points are not full sentences, start them with a lower-case letter and end the last one with a full stop.

At this year's Monster Convention, guests will have the opportunity to:

- *practise their scary skills*
- *meet other monsters*
- *have a rest from non-monsters screaming and running away from them.*

If the bullet points are full sentences, you start them with a capital letter and end them with a full stop.

Here are some of the opportunities on offer at this year's Monster Convention:

- *You can practise your scary skills.*
- *You can meet other monsters.*
- *You can enjoy a rest from non-monsters screaming and running away from you.*

2. Turn these passages of text into correctly punctuated bullet point lists. Don't forget capital letters where necessary, too.

the delicious food on offer at the annual monster convention includes the following slug supreme eyeball delight putrefying pizza dangerous doughnuts

_____
_____
_____
_____

there is a packed programme of exciting events for monsters attending the convention you can visit the nearby haunted house creepy hall you can listen to visiting speakers from transylvania and monsterville you can take part in creepy debates and discussions

_____
_____
_____
_____
_____
_____

Room For One More

How difficult it was to sleep in that strange bed! She wrestled with the duvet and thumped the pillow; she turned her back on the flimsy curtains; she wished she had never come up to London.

At midnight she heard the grandfather clock whirr and strike; and then she heard the gravel in the driveway crunch. At once she jumped out of bed and crossed the room and just peeped between the curtains.

What she could see was a gleaming black hearse. But there was no coffin in it, and no flowers. No, the hearse was packed out with living people: a crush of talking, laughing, living people.

Then the driver of the hearse looked straight up at her, as she peeped between the curtains.

"There's room for one more." That's what he said. She could hear his voice quite clearly. Then she tugged the curtains so they crossed over, and ran back across the room, and jumped into bed, and pulled the duvet up over her head. And when she woke up the next morning, she really wasn't sure whether it was all a dream or not.

That day, she went shopping. In the big store, she did Levis Jeanswear on the fifth floor; she did Adidas Sportswear and that was on the sixth floor; and then she did cosmetics and that was on the seventh floor. Carrying two bags in each hand, she walked over to the lift. But when the bell pinged and the doors opened, she saw the lift was already jammed full with people.

The lift attendant looked straight at her as she stood there with her bags. "There's room for one more," he said. And his face was the face of the driver of the hearse.

"No," she said quickly. "No, I'll walk down."

Then the lift door closed with a clang. At once there was a kind of grating screech, and a terrible rattling, then a huge double thud.

The lift in the big store dropped from top to bottom of the shaft, and every single person in it was killed.

Kevin Crossley-Holland

1. At what time did the clock strike? _____

2. What was in the back of the hearse? _____

3. On what floor did the main character end her shopping? _____

4. Why did the lift attendant look familiar to her? _____

5. Which departments in the shop did she visit? _____
_____

6. How was the main character sleeping? Support your answer with evidence from the text.
_____

7. *She heard the gravel in the driveway crunch.* Why does the author tell us that the gravel crunches?
_____

8. *She tugged the curtains so they crossed over, and ran back across the room, and jumped into bed, and pulled the duvet up over her head.* Why has the author used so many commas in this sentence?
_____

9. Find and copy two statements where the author attempts to build suspense or a sense of fear.
_____
_____

10. What is your opinion of this as a scary story? Support your opinion with evidence from the text.
_____
_____

Children at work

Read the passage, then answer the questions.

Coal mines were vital for Britain's survival in Victorian times, because people used coal as a source of power, both for heating their homes and for running machines such as steam engines and factory equipment.

In coal mines there were three main jobs open to children: trapper, hurrier and pusher. In early Victorian times, children were hired to work down in the mine from the age of six. On average they worked from five in the morning until approximately five in the afternoon. Their only day off was Sunday, and they earned the equivalent of about ten pence a week for their work.

Children who worked as trappers in mines were required to sit in the dark all day, waiting until they heard the sound of a mine cart coming. Then they opened the door to let the cart through. Trappers were mostly small children, because the doors and passages inside the mine were only 26 inches (about 66 centimetres) high.

Children also worked as hurriers. The hurriers had to help load the mine carts with coal. Once a mine cart was loaded, the hurrier would put on a huge leather belt which had a chain attached to it. Once the belt was secure, the hurrier would get down on his hands and knees and pull the cart along, using the chain. This process could be repeated up to sixteen times a day.

Occasionally, hurriers would have a pusher to help with the cart. Pushers used their heads to push the cart when a hurrier was not strong enough to pull the cart independently. The pusher would be positioned at the rear of the cart.

Working in a mine was not only exhausting and difficult; it was highly dangerous as well. Many miners – children as well as adults – died in accidents. Spending so much time in cramped and unhealthy conditions meant that miners' health suffered. People became increasingly shocked by the conditions that children aged were working in underground. In 1842 a law was passed to prevent women and children aged under 10 from working in mines. By 1900, no boys under 13 were allowed to be miners.

Based on a text by Stephen Moore

1. Why were coal mines so important in Victorian times?

_____

_____

2. How many hours per day did children have to work in coal mines, during early Victorian times?

_____

3. Why might a child who worked in a coal mine look forward to Sunday?

_____

4. Why did hurriers have big leather belts?

_____

5. Why might a tall child or an adult have found it difficult to be a trapper?

_____

_____

6. If you were a Victorian child working in a coal mine, which of the three jobs mentioned in the text would you *least* like to have, and why?

_____

_____

7. Name *two* ways in which working in a coal mine could be dangerous.

_____

8. Why do you think the government eventually decided to pass a law to stop young children being employed in coal mines?

_____

_____

The Secret Garden

Read the passage from the story. Then answer these questions.

When Mary Lennox was sent to Misselthwaite Manor to live with her uncle, everybody said she was the most disagreeable-looking child ever seen. It was true, too. She had a little thin face and a little thin body, thin light hair and a sour expression. Her hair was yellow, and her face was yellow because she had been born in India and had always been ill in one way or another. Her father had held a position under the English Government and had always been busy and ill himself, and her mother had been a great beauty who cared only to go to parties and amuse herself with carefree people. She had not wanted a little girl at all, and when Mary was born she handed her over to the care of an Ayah*, who was made to understand that if she wished to please the Memsahib** she must keep the child out of sight as much as possible. So, when she was a sickly, fretful, ugly little baby she was kept out of the way, and when she became a sickly, fretful, toddling thing she was kept out of the way also. She never remembered seeing familiarly anything but the dark faces of her Ayah and the other native servants, and as they always obeyed her and gave her her own way in everything, because the Memsahib would be angry if she was disturbed by her crying, by the time she was six years old she was as tyrannical and selfish a little pig as ever lived.

Frances Hodgson Burnett

*Ayah = servant; nanny
**Memsahib = mistress of the house

1. Why did Mary Lennox go to Misselthwaite Manor?

   _____

2. Why did Mary have a yellow face?

   a. because she was suntanned after living in India. ☐

   b. because she was often ill. ☐

   c. because she was jealous. ☐

3. Underline the phrase which best describes Mary's mother.

   beautiful and selfish   fretful and sickly   cruel and terrifying

4. Write a sentence to describe Mary's Ayah.

   _____

   _____

5. Why do you think Mary was *tyrannical and selfish* by the time she was six years old?

   _____

6. Mary had always lived in India before she went to Misselthwaite Manor in Yorkshire. Judging by the evidence in this passage, how do you think Mary will feel about going to Misselthwaite?

   _____

   _____

7. Why do you think Mary's father didn't look after her and make sure she was all right?

   _____

8. Do you feel sorry for Mary, based on the evidence in this passage? Explain why or why not.

   _____

   _____

Race against time

Read the passage from the playscript. Then answer the questions.

The scene is a suburban street corner on a sunny Saturday afternoon. Cameron is waiting for someone. He looks anxious.

Cameron: *(to himself)* Where is he? Where is he? He said he'd be here by now. What if he doesn't turn up? No – don't even think about that! He must get here soon – he must!

(Mrs Turner, Cameron's class teacher, comes along. She spots Cameron and stops.)

Mrs Turner: *(concerned)* Cameron? Is everything all right?

Cameron: What? Oh, er … hi, Mrs Turner. I'm fine. Everything's fine. Honest.

Mrs Turner: Oh well, if you're sure, Cameron. I'll leave you to it. *(She walks on.)*

(Jamie comes running round the corner in a huge rush. He almost knocks Cameron over.)

Jamie: Cameron, mate! Sorry – I didn't see you there. Are you OK?

Cameron: I am now! What took you so long? I've been going mad thinking you weren't coming after all!

Jamie: Hey! Would I let you down? Anyway, we'd better run if we want to get to the park before the others get there.

(The boys start running towards the park.)

Cameron: *(panting)* But what if the others are there already? Or if they've already found the stuff and gone home?

Jamie: You worry too much! Leave it to me, Cam. It'll be fine, you'll see.

(They get to the park.)

Cameron: Come on – we'd better get to the hollow tree fast. I can see Ben and Jamal heading that way. We've got to get there before them!

Jamie: Don't worry – we'll get there easily! Ben and Jamal are really slow runners. And anyway, they don't know exactly where the stuff is hidden. Even if they do get there first, I bet I can put them off the scent.

Cameron: OK … if you say so. How about you distract them, while I get the stuff out of the hollow tree?

Jamie: Sounds like a good plan. Come on – quick!

1. What is the setting at the start of the playscript?

   _____

2. What is the setting at the end?

   _____

3. Why is Cameron anxious at the start of the playscript?

   _____

4. How do you think Cameron feels when Mrs Turner stops to talk to him? Quote evidence from the text to explain how you know.

   _____

5. What kind of person is Jamie? How do you know?

   _____

6. Think of three words to describe Cameron, based on what we know about him from the playscript.

   _____

7. Why do Jamie and Cameron have to run to the park?

   _____

8. Who else is trying to get to the hollow tree?

   _____

9. What do you think might be hidden in the hollow tree?

   _____

10. Write the conversation between Jamie, Ben and Jamal when Jamie tries to distract the others so that Cameron can get the stuff out of the hollow tree.

   _____

   _____

   _____

Caribbean folk tale

Read the story, then answer the questions.

Oral version of a Caribbean folk tale

Let me tell 'ee the story of Rose Hall – that was one big house! – the best in Jamaica, folks say. Well, it was owned by John Palmer – he be one of them colonial planters – worth a fortune a was and all from the hard work of black brothers and sisters. *(Sadly.)* Slaves, they was. Well. His troubles began when he brought a bride back to Rose Hall – that was 1820, I mind. At first they was happy enough, but Annie, well a was only 18, and she soon got tired o' that lardy husband – well, he was old man, do yo see, and she was young girl – so she takes up wi' a young man – a slave, he was. When her husband find out, he go stark staring mad and they had real bad argument. *(Frowns.)* Soon after, John Palmer, he was found dead. Well, they blame Annie. They say that she got her lover to strangle him. Soon after that she had the slave whip to death so as to get rid of the only witness. Well, Annie was master now – and a cruel one! *(Gestures as if using a rod.)* She rule the estate with a rod of iron – ooh and was she bad to her slaves! One day she whip a slave so bad that his back was ripped open 'til yo could see the bone! *(Shakes head.)* That boy was so wild wi' pain he broke loose and tried to strangle her. Ha, ha – the best part is that when she cry for help, the other slaves, they help him – not her! They put a mattress on her and jump on it until she was suffocated to death – serve her right too! *(Grins and nods.)* They say she haunt the place now. *(Frowns.)* Well, guess what – that old place – Rose Hall – was a ruin for years, but now they've done it all up – the Jamaican government – for tourists – ha ha – but yo wouldn't catch me goin' there *(waves hand)* – no, no, not with the ghost of old Annie and all!

1. Who was Annie?
   a. one of the slaves who worked on the plantation ☐
   b. the wife of the plantation owner, John Palmer ☐
   c. the narrator of the story ☐

2. What evidence can you find in the story to suggest that the narrator of the story is black?

   _____

3. What does the narrator say has happened to Rose Hall now?

   _____

4. Why wouldn't the narrator want to go to Rose Hall?

   _____

5. Do you agree with the narrator about this? Explain why, or why not.

   _____

6. How did Annie die?

   _____

7. Do you think she deserved her fate? Explain why, or why not.

   _____

8. Write out three quotations from the text that show this is an oral story rather than a written one.

   _____

   _____

   _____

The *Lusitania* disaster

Read the passage, then answer the questions.

The *Lusitania* disaster of 1915 was like an action replay of the *Titanic* disaster of three years earlier. The two ships even looked alike, both having four tall funnels and two tall masts fore and aft.

The *Lusitania* sailed from New York to Liverpool with a full load of passengers, including Canadian soldiers, and a cargo of munitions. She was the largest liner afloat at the time (though smaller than the *Titanic*). She was also the holder of the transatlantic speed record. She was much faster than any German U–boat so it was believed that if she kept moving, there would be little danger. Just after 2:00pm on May 7, the ship changed course toward the Irish Sea and the coast of Ireland came into view. Suddenly, a warning was shouted from the bridge, "There is a torpedo coming, Sir!"

Soon after, there was a violent explosion in the *Lusitania* hull. It was a direct hit from a German submarine about 700 yards away. The ship sank so quickly that most lifeboats could not be lowered in time. Within 18 minutes the liner had gone down and 1198 of the 1959 passengers died – almost as many as died in the *Titanic* disaster.

The German captain, after watching the disaster through his periscope, wrote in his log, "The ship stops immediately and quickly heels to starboard. Great confusion... Lifeboats being cleared and lowered to water. Many boats crowded... immediately fill and sink."

The German government said that the ship had been sunk because it was carrying soldiers and munitions. However, public opinion was outraged, and it was one of the reasons why America eventually joined the war against Germany.

1. What was the date and time of the *Lusitania* disaster?

    _____

2. Why do you think the author says it was *like an action replay* of the Titanic *disaster*?

    _____

    _____

3. What caused the *Lusitania* to sink?
    a. It developed a bad leak when it struck an iceberg. ☐
    b. It was hit by a torpedo from a German submarine. ☐
    c. It ran aground on the coast of Ireland. ☐

4. Where was the *Lusitania* sailing from and to, on her final voyage?

    _____

5. How many passengers died in the disaster?

    _____

6. Underline the phrase that best describes the *Lusitania*.

    a fast and unsinkable U-boat

    a heavily laden German U-boat

    a large and record-breaking liner

7. Why couldn't many of the passengers escape in the *Lusitania's* lifeboats?

    _____

8. Why do you think public opinion was outraged by the sinking of the *Lusitania*?

    _____

    _____

    _____

My Dad, Your Dad

My dad's fatter than your dad,
Yes, my dad's fatter than yours:
If he eats any more he won't fit in the house,
He'll have to live out of doors.

Yes, but my dad's balder than your dad,
Yes, my dad's balder, O.K.,
He's only got two hairs left on his head
And both are turning grey.

Ah, but my dad's thicker than your dad,
My dad's thicker, alright.
He has to look at his watch to see
If it's noon or the middle of the night.

Yes, but my dad's more boring than your dad.
If he ever starts counting sheep
When he can't get to sleep at night, he finds
It's the sheep that go to sleep.

But my dad doesn't mind your dad.
Mine quite likes yours too.
I suppose *they* don't always think much of US!
That's true, I suppose, that's true.

Kit Wright

1. Why do you think the writer chose to use italic text (*like this*) for some verses, and normal text for other verses?

    _____

2. What evidence does one of the narrators give for his dad being the thickest?

    _____

3. Which of the following is true about the rhyme scheme of the poem?
    a. Lines 2 and 4 rhyme in each verse. ☐
    b. Lines 1 and 3 rhyme in each verse. ☐
    c. Line 1 always rhymes with line 2, and line 3 always rhymes with line 4. ☐

4. Underline the description that best fits the poem.

    sad and thoughtful   funny and cheeky   detailed and descriptive

5. What evidence does one of the narrators give for his dad being the most boring?

    _____

6. In what ways is the last verse different from all the other verses in the poem?

    _____

7. Which verse do you think is the funniest? Give your reasons.

    _____

8. Write a short conversation between the two dads, about their children. What might they say? It doesn't have to rhyme.

    _____

    _____

    _____

    _____

Iroquois creation myth

Read the passage; then answer the questions.

nce, before the world we know existed, the Spirits lived on an island, floating in the sky, where the ruler of the Sky Island, Great Spirit, had a wife who was expecting his baby. One night she had a dream that the Celestial Tree, from which grew all the fruit and flowers for the island, was uprooted. She told her husband of the dream. Realising that the dream was a powerful message, he at once uprooted the tree, leaving a great hole in the middle of the island. But when his curious wife peered into the hole, she slipped and tumbled through, down towards the waters below. As she slipped, she grabbed a handful of seeds from the branches of the Celestial Tree.

Animals already existed in the water. So, far below the floating island, two birds saw the Sky Woman fall. They caught her on their backs, just before she plunged into the water, and brought her to the other animals. Trying to help the woman, they dived into the water to get mud from the bottom of the seas. One after another the animals tried and failed. Finally, Little Toad tried and returned with a single mouthful of mud. The other animals took it and spread it on the back of Big Turtle. The mud began to grow and grow and grow until it became the whole world.

Then the woman stepped onto the land. She sprinkled the seeds onto the ground and from them grew all the plants of the earth.

Then Sky Woman gave birth to a daughter, who married the West Wind and in time, gave birth to twin sons. She named one Sapling. He grew up to be kind and caring. She named the other Flint and his heart was as cold as his name. They grew quickly and began filling the earth with their creations.

Sapling created all that is good. He taught the birds to sing and fish to leap. He made rivers, soft rain and rainbows.

However, Flint was jealous and tried to destroy Sapling's work and made all that is bad. He made the rapids in the rivers. He created poisonous plants. He created monsters which his brother drove beneath the Earth.

At last, Sapling decided Flint should be driven out. He challenged him to a fight and Flint was beaten. As he was a god, Flint could not die, so he was banished to live under the land. He still shows his anger in the eruptions of volcanoes.

1. Do you think this story tells how the world was really created?

   Yes ☐   No ☐

2. Why did Sky Woman fall?

   _____

   _____

3. How does Sky Woman create trees and plants?

   _____

   _____

4. How does evil come into the new world?

   _____

   _____

5. Who defeats the evil? How?

   _____

   _____

6. What happens to Flint?

   _____

   _____

   _____

   _____

The Lost Angels

Read the poem, then answer the questions.

In a fish tank in France
we discovered the lost angels,
fallen from heaven and floating now
on imaginary tides.
And all along the sides of the tank,
faces peered, leered at them,
laughing, pouting,
pointing, shouting,
while hung above their heads, a sign,
'Ne pas plonger les mains dans le basin.'
Don't put your hands in the tank
– the turtles bite seriously.
And who can blame them,
these creatures with angels' wings,
drifting past like alien craft.
Who knows what signals they send
through an imitation ocean,
out of sight of sky,
out of touch with stars?

Dream on, lost angels,
then one day, one glorious day,
you'll flap your wings
and fly again.

Brian Moses

1. What are the lost angels in the poem?

    a. fish ☐

    b. angels that have fallen from heaven ☐

    c. turtles ☐

2. Why do you think the poet uses the phrase *lost angels* to describe them?

    _____

3. Whose do you think are the faces that *peered, leered at them, laughing, pouting, pointing, shouting*?

    _____

4. Copy out two quotations from the text that use figurative language.

    _____

    _____

5. Why does the poet say the angels are floating *on imaginary tides* and through an *imitation ocean*?

    _____

6. Does the illustration help you understand the poem? Explain your views.

    _____

7. How do you think the poet wants us to feel about the lost angels? Explain your views by quoting from the text.

    _____

8. What do you think the angels' wings are, really?

    _____

    _____

Visit Venice by train

Visit Venice by train

Imagine a leisurely journey in luxurious surroundings.
Imagine watching a fascinating landscape slide past your window.
Imagine arriving in Venice, refreshed and delighted.
Wouldn't you want to begin your holiday like that?

TerrificTrainTravel.com will organise every aspect of your journey. You arrive
renewed, relaxed and ready to begin your Venetian adventure.
What better way could there possibly be?

100% of our customers tell us they are delighted with our service.
89% of our customers travel with us every year!
All our customers receive personal service!
Why not join them and start a holiday of a life time in style?

For a limited period only!
Book before 11th March and receive a complimentary travel pack.

1. Underline the description that best fits the poem.

    instructional   persuasive   descriptive

2. Rhetorical questions are questions which are asked without expecting an answer. Find and underline three rhetorical questions in the text on page 104.

3. What statistics are used in the text?

    _____

4. Why do you think the author decided to use these statistics?

    _____

5. Why does the author use words like *leisurely*, *luxurious*, *fascinating*, *refreshed* and *delighted*?

    _____

6. How does the author encourage readers to respond quickly?

    _____

7. Does the text succeed in making you feel the holiday described would be good? Explain why, or why not.

    _____

    _____

8. What is the name of the travel company responsible for this text?

    _____

9. Why do you think the author decided to include pictures as well as words? Are the pictures helpful? Explain your opinion.

    _____

    _____

Choosing your words carefully

When you are writing a piece of text, there are a few things you always need to bear in mind.
- Who do you want to read the text? (**audience**)
- What message do you want them to get from the text? (**purpose**)
- What are texts like this normally like? (**text features**)

Thinking about these things in advance will really help you to choose the right vocabulary for your piece of writing – and it can even help you choose the right grammar and structure, too.

1. **Look at the short pieces of text in the table. For each one, say who you think the audience is, what the purpose is, and what the key features of the text are.**

Text	Audience	Purpose	Features
Come to beautiful Balton! Enjoy the glorious sunshine on our secluded beach! Why wait to begin your dream holiday?	People who might be interested in buying a holiday.	To persuade people to buy a holiday.	Imperative language (*Come!*), exaggerated language (*glorious, secluded*), rhetorical question (*Why wait...?*).
Mr Twinkletoes was a tiny elf. He lived all alone at the bottom of Martha's garden. Martha's mummy didn't know he existed, but Martha and the elf were best friends.			
Hedgehogs and porcupines share some important characteristics. For example, they both have spines, or quills.			

2. **Plan an instructional text for younger children, telling them how to do something you know how to do yourself. You can choose any topic you like – for example, you could tell them the rules of a game, or give them instructions for making some food or drink. Use the spider diagram below to collect your ideas.**

Key things I want the reader to know:

_____

_____

_____

_____

Equipment the reader will need:

_____

_____

_____

_____

What is the text about?

_____

_____

Text features of instructional texts that I will use:

_____

_____

_____

_____

_____

Tricky aspects the reader will need to watch out for:

_____

_____

_____

_____

_____

Write a leaflet

The Healthy Schools Initiative is writing a leaflet about how primary schools can encourage a healthy lifestyle. The organisation has already created pages on physical education (PE), after-school activities and healthier menus for school meals. The Healthy Schools Initiative would like you to plan and write the page dedicated to encouraging children aged 7 to 11 to eat fruit at morning break time, rather than less healthy alternatives.

1. Fill in the spider diagram to help you plan your page. Use words and short phrases, not whole sentences. Remember to think about the *audience*, *purpose* and *text features*.

Reasons why eating fruit is good for you:

_____
_____
_____
_____
_____

Reasons why children might enjoy eating fruit:

_____
_____
_____

Title for the page:

_____
_____

Text features of persuasive leaflets that I will use:

_____
_____
_____
_____

What do I want the reader to do after reading the page?

_____
_____
_____
_____

2.   Use the writing frame below to write a draft of your leaflet page.

heading

picture

Tell the reader why eating fruit is a) good for them and b) fun.

Don't forget persuasive language.

You could use a bullet point list.

You could use bold text or capitals.

Describing settings

There are lots of different ways authors help readers to visualise the *setting* of a story. Sometimes there is no direct description – just a few important details. For example: *The kitchen was quiet except for the swish, swish of the washing machine.* Here, the author hasn't described the kitchen in detail, because the reader doesn't need to know exactly what it looks like. There is enough to help the reader imagine it.

Sometimes the author does need to describe the setting in detail – for example, if the setting helps to convey the atmosphere of the story, or if it might be unfamiliar to the reader.

1. Write the opening paragraph for a story set in your school. You don't have to describe the setting in detail, but add a few details that will help your reader to imagine it.

_____

_____

_____

_____

2. Write the opening paragraph for a story set on a strange alien planet. You will need to describe this setting in a bit more detail, because it will be unfamiliar to the reader. Try to put in some details that help the reader to imagine the setting and atmosphere.

_____

_____

_____

_____

_____

_____

3. **Choose one of the settings cards below. Then write the opening of a story that takes place in your chosen setting. Here are some things to think about:**
   - **Is your setting likely to be familiar to the reader already?**
   - **Do you need to describe the setting completely, or just add a few key details?**
   - **Do you want to use the setting to help the reader understand the atmosphere of the story?**

Write your story opening here.

_____

_____

_____

_____

_____

_____

Conveying atmosphere

Authors convey atmosphere in lots of different ways. Sometimes, the way they describe how their story setting **looks** helps to convey atmosphere. Look at pages 110 and 111 for some examples of this.

Authors can also use the other senses to help the reader enter into the atmosphere of their writing. In the poem below, the nineteenth-century poet John Clare uses **sounds** to convey atmosphere.

1.   **Underline the words and phrases in the poem that you think convey atmosphere best.**

Pleasant Sounds

The rustling of leaves under the feet in woods

and under hedges;

The crumping of cat-ice and snow down wood-rides,

narrow lanes, and every street causeway;

Rustling through a wood or rather rushing, while the

wind halloos in the oak-top like thunder;

The rustle of birds' wings startled from their nests or

flying unseen into the bushes;

The whizzing of larger birds overhead in a wood,

such as crows, puddocks, buzzards;

The trample of robins and woodlarks on the brown

leaves, and the patter of squirrels on the green moss;

The fall of an acorn on the ground, the pattering of

nuts on the hazel branches as they fall from ripeness;

The flirt of the groundlark's wing from the stubbles –

how sweet such pictures on dewy mornings,

when the dew flashes from its brown feathers!

2. Make a list of the sounds that *you* often hear at a particular time of day – for example, in the early morning, or at lunchtime at school, or at bedtime…

_____

_____

_____

_____

_____

_____

3. Take some of the ideas you have written above, and use them to write an atmospheric paragraph about the time of day you chose. You can add other details to convey atmosphere as well as sounds. For example, what can you see, smell, taste, touch…?

_____

_____

_____

_____

_____

_____

_____

_____

Writing about characters

1. Read this extract from *The Borrowers* by Mary Norton. Highlight or underline words and phrases that help us to get to know the character of Mrs May. Use one colour for what she says, another for what she does, and another for the author's descriptions.

It was Mrs May who first told me about them. No, not me. How could it have been me – a wild, untidy, self-willed little girl who stared with angry eyes and was said to crunch her teeth? Kate, she should have been called. Yes, that was it, Kate. Not that the name matters much either way: she barely comes into the story.

Mrs May lived in two rooms in Kate's parents' house in London. She was, I think, some kind of relation. Her bedroom was on the first floor, and her sitting-room was a room which, as part of the house, was called 'the breakfast-room'. Now 'breakfast-rooms' are all right in the morning when the sun streams in on the toast and marmalade, but by afternoon they seem to vanish a little and to fill with a strange silvery light, their own twilight; there is a kind of sadness in them then, but as a child it was a sadness Kate liked. She would creep in to Mrs May just before tea-time and Mrs May would teach her to crochet.

Mrs May was old, her joints were stiff, and she was – not strict exactly; but she had that inner certainty which does instead. Kate was never 'wild' with Mrs May, nor untidy, nor self-willed; and Mrs May taught her many things besides crochet: how to wind wool into an egg-shaped ball; how to run-and-fell and plan a darn; how to tidy a drawer and to lay, like a blessing, above the contents, a sheet of rustling tissue against the dust.

"Why so quiet, child?" asked Mrs May one day, when Kate was sitting hunched and idle upon the hassock. "What's the matter with you? Have you lost your tongue?"

"No," said Kate, pulling at her shoe button, "I've lost the crochet hook ..." (they were making a bedquilt – in woollen squares: there were thirty still to do). "I know where I put it," she went on hastily; "I put it on the bottom shelf of the book-case just beside my bed."

"On the bottom shelf?" repeated Mrs May, her own needle flicking steadily in the firelight. "Near the floor?"

"Yes," said Kate, "but I looked on the floor. Under the rug. Everywhere. The wool was still there though. Just where I'd left it."

"Oh dear," exclaimed Mrs May lightly, "don't say they're in this house too!"

"That what are?" asked Kate.

"The Borrowers," said Mrs May; and in the half light she seemed to smile.

2. In your own words, write a short character description of Mrs May based on the words and phrases you underlined on page 114.

Mrs May

_____

_____

_____

_____

_____

_____

_____

3. Now write a short piece of text about a character of your own. Tell the reader what they say and what they do, as well as describing them. The character can be based on someone you know in real life, or you can make them up.

_____

_____

_____

_____

_____

_____

Composition

Using dialogue to keep the plot moving

Writers use *dialogue* in stories for lots of different reasons. Here are just a few:

a.   to help the reader imagine the characters and understand what they are like

b.   to add variety and keep the reader interested

c.   to provide clues about the characters' thoughts, feelings and reasons for doing things

d.   to help keep the plot moving.

1.   Look at the pieces of *dialogue* below and decide which of the reasons above fits each example best. Write a., b., c. or d. by each example. You can write more than one letter if more than one reason fits.

a.   "I'm not sure," said Michael. "I don't think that's a good idea.
     What if Mum gets really upset?"   _____

b.   "I've been saving my pocket money," said Donna, "and now
     I've got nearly enough to buy…"   _____

c.   "Listen, Marta," said Kwezi. "We've got to escape – and I've got a plan.
     Meet me by the back door at three o'clock – and bring some rope."   _____

2.   Imagine you are writing a story about two children who decide to do something extraordinary – it can be anything you like. Write a short conversation between them, where one of the children explains to the other what they are going to do. The dialogue should show the reader what is going to happen next, and help keep the plot moving.

_____

_____

_____

_____

_____

Now you are going to create dialogue for some new characters: Molly and George.

The story so far…

Molly and George are in dispute over George's paper aeroplane. Molly has objected to George expecting her to fetch and carry for him. Their disagreement seems to be resolved until Molly's turn at throwing the plane ends up with it landing – smack – in George's face.

3. Write the last things Molly and George said to each other.

"

_____

_____, said Molly, throwing the plane.

"

_____

_____, said George, rubbing his nose.

4. A new character enters the scene. Decide who the new character is and what each character will say to introduce him or her into the story. Remember to use the correct punctuation.

_____

_____

_____

5. Fill in the chart below to show what Molly and George each thought about the new character based on what they said above.

Molly	George

Composition

Linking paragraphs

Read the timeline below. You are going to use it to write a short biography of Albert Einstein.

The life of Albert Einstein: a timeline

1879: Albert Einstein is born to Hermann and Pauline Einstein in Ulm, a town near Munich, Germany.

1894: The Einsteins to Pavia, Italy. Albert stays to finish school in Munich. He only lasts a month without his family and then joins them in Italy.

1895: Albert sits a university entrance exam but fails on the arts section. His family send him to the Swiss town of Aarau to finish high school.

1896: Albert graduates high school and enrols in a polytechnic in Zurich.

1898: Albert meets fellow student Mileva Maric and falls in love.

1900: Albert graduates from the polytechnic.

1901: Albert becomes a Swiss citizen.

1902: Hermann Einstein becomes ill and dies.

1903: Albert and Mileva marry.

1904: Albert and Mileva have a son called Hans Albert.

1905: Albert Einstein publishes an article entitled 'On the electrodynamics of moving bodies' in a leading German physics journal. He applies his theory to mass and energy and formulates the famous equation $e=mc^2$.

1910: The Einsteins have a second son, Eduard.

1911: Albert and his family move to Prague where Albert is given a professorship at the university there.

1912: The family then moves to Zurich where Albert is again made a professor.

1914: Einstein become director of the Kaiser Wilhelm institute in Berlin. He and Mileva begin divorce proceedings.

1915: The general theory of relativity is finished.

1919: Albert remarries – his second wife is called Elsa. A solar eclipse proves that Einstein's theory of relativity works.

1921: Albert Einstein is awarded the Nobel Prize for physics.

1. Read the paragraph below, and then continue the biography from 1895 onwards, using information from the timeline. Don't forget to write in clear paragraphs, using words and phrases such as *then*, *after that*, *this*, *firstly*, *later* to help the reader understand how the ideas in your paragraphs are linked.

Albert Einstein was born in 1879 in Ulm, Germany. He was the son of Hermann and Pauline Einstein. The Einstein family moved to Pavia, Italy, in 1894 – leaving the 15-year-old Albert in Munich to finish school. However, he lasted only a month before joining his family in Italy.

At the age of 16, Albert sat a university entrance exam. _____

_____

_____

_____

_____

_____

_____

_____

_____

_____

_____

_____

_____

_____

Writing instructions

1. Read this letter and then present the information again, giving clear instructions. Remember to give your writing a heading, to list the ingredients and then write out the instructions for making a jelly.

Sam wrote a letter to her friend describing how she made a jelly for her mum.

"I thought I'd give my mum a surprise, so I got a packet of jelly from the cupboard and read what I had to do. I boiled a kettle of water, but I couldn't find a measuring jug so I just guessed the pint of water. Anyway, I poured the water over the jelly and stirred it until it had melted. I thought I would put it in the fridge to set quickly. When it was supper time I got my jelly – it had set and looked a lovely colour. Unfortunately, when my mum came to serve it, she had to cut it with a knife! She said that I had not added enough water. Still, it tasted great."

_____

Ingredients _____

_____

Method _____

_____

_____

_____

_____

_____

_____

_____

A newspaper article

The headline for this photograph suggests the event was great fun.

Water weekly   Wednesday 23 October

The crazy boat race

1. **Write an article about the picture. Here are some ideas to help you.**
   - **How many teams?**
   - **Team names?**
   - **What sort of boats?**
   - **How far to race?**
   - **What happened during the race?**
   - **Which team won?**

_____

_____

_____

_____

_____

_____

2. **Write a caption for the picture.**

_____

An encyclopedia article

Cross-section through the Earth

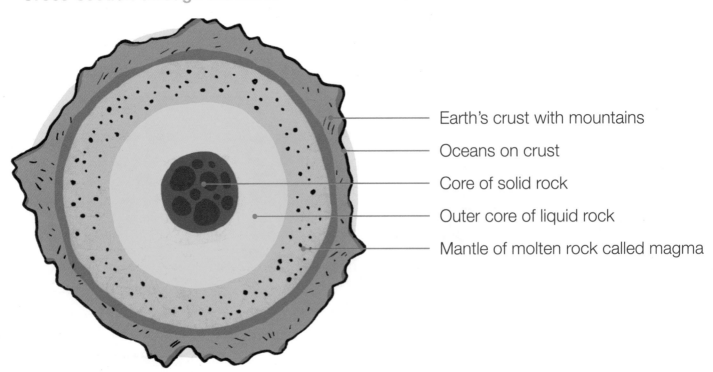

Earth's crust with mountains

Oceans on crust

Core of solid rock

Outer core of liquid rock

Mantle of molten rock called magma

1.   **Using the diagram above, write an encyclopedia entry describing a cross-section through the Earth.**

You could start your entry:

EARTH

Inside the Earth

People once believed that the Earth was flat, but today...

_____

_____

_____

_____

_____

_____

_____